© 1995 Brimar Publishing Inc.
338 Saint Antoine St. East
Montreal, Canada H2Y 1A3
Tel. (514) 954-1441
Fax (514) 954-5086

Graphic Design: Zapp
Photography: Nathalie Dumouchel
Food Preparation/Stylist: Josée Robitaille
Assistant Stylist: Louis Hudon
Props courtesy of: Arthur Quentin
                  Pier 1 Imports
                  Stokes

Pictured on the front cover:
Pasta Primavera *(see recipe, page 102)*

Primo is a Registered Trademark of
Primo Foods Limited
Woodbridge, Ontario
Canada, L4L 8M4

All recipes in the Primo *Family Favourites*
cookbook were developed and tested
in the Primo Kitchens.

Primo Kitchens Manager: Carolyn Gall
Recipe Testing/Development: Lesleigh Landry
Project Manager: Rob Steele
Project Assistant: Margaret Tauriello

Nutrition information is available for all recipes
presented in this cookbook. Please forward any
requests, questions or comments to:

Primo Family Favourites
P.O. Box 56559
Woodbridge Postal Outlet
Woodbridge, Ontario
L4L 8V3

ISBN 2-89433-182-7

Printed in Canada

Family FAVOURITES

Good cooking begins with the Primo family of fine Italian foods and the Primo *Family Favourites* cookbook. Primo's passion for great tasting recipes is showcased in this cookbook which features traditional Italian family favourites and more contemporary recipe ideas.

The Primo *Family Favourites* cookbook is more than just another pasta cookbook. Primo *Family Favourites* is a complete cookbook which includes delicious pasta and non-pasta recipe ideas for appetizers, soups, salads, main courses, and desserts.

All 119 delicious recipes in the Primo *Family Favourites* cookbook are easy to prepare. Helpful icons identify recipes as Quick-and-Easy, Classic Italian, and Low Fat, and selected recipes include step-by-step technique photography to help make preparation that much easier. You will also find pasta pointers, cooking tips, helpful hints and serving suggestions to make your meal a success with family and friends.

Primo *Family Favourites* truly offers something for everyone and we are sure this cookbook will be a favourite in your kitchen for many years.

From our family to yours ... enjoy!

THE PRIMO FOODS STORY

Primo Poloniato came to Canada in 1920 at the age of six from a small town in Italy called Montebelluna. Primo means "first" in Italian, and he was named Primo because he was the first born in the family. In the late 1940's Primo started his own business as a small food distributor selling fresh bread, biscuits, salami and cheese from the back of an old truck. In 1954, Primo purchased a small pasta manufacturing company and Primo Foods was born.

Primo Foods has grown into Canada's largest Italian food company with a presence across the country. Primo Foods now offers consumers a complete line of Italian food products: pasta, pasta sauces, beans, tomatoes, oils, soups, biscuits, grated cheeses, pizza sauces, rice and much more. Primo is committed to delivering the highest quality pasta and Italian food products to our consumers. This commitment is evident in the delicious recipes found in this cookbook.

ICON DESCRIPTORS

Primo *Family Favourites* has developed the following icons to help make recipe selection easier.

QUICK AND EASY
Recipes with this symbol can be prepared and served in 45 minutes or less. Look for this symbol for fast, delicious meals on busy weeknights.

CLASSIC ITALIAN
Recipes are inspired from various regions in Italy. Primo has developed the recipes with an eye for maintaining the integrity of these original old world favourites.

LOW FAT
Primo presents this icon to help you quickly identify recipes which are lower in total fat. For appetizers and desserts, the recipes will have less than 5 g of total fat per serving. For soups and salads the total fat content is under 15 g and entrées with this symbol will have less than 18 g of fat per serving. Calculations do not take into consideration optional ingredients or garnishes. For more detailed nutrition information, please write to Primo at the address given in the front of the cookbook.

CONTENTS

INTRODUCTION
➤ 6 ◄

APPETIZERS AND HORS D'OEUVRES
➤ 15 ◄

SUPER SOUPS
➤ 37 ◄

SPLENDID SALADS
➤ 51 ◄

BEEF, PORK AND POULTRY
➤ 69 ◄

FROM THE SEA
➤ 87 ◄

VEGETABLE FAVOURITES
➤ 101 ◄

CREAMY CREATIONS
➤ 123 ◄

HEARTY SIMMERED SAUCES
➤ 131 ◄

BEAUTIFULLY BAKED CASSEROLES
➤ 145 ◄

DELICIOUS DESSERTS
➤ 173 ◄

INDEX
➤ 190 ◄

PASTA PERFECTION

STORAGE:

•Unopened packages of Primo pasta will keep for up to 2 years, after which they begin to lose optimum flavour and texture. Opened pastas stored in a sealed container will keep up to 1 year. Clear bottles and jars filled with different cuts of pasta can add a decorative touch to any kitchen countertop!

COOKING:

•Cook 2 oz (50 g) dry pasta per person for an appetizer or side dish portion, and 3-4 oz (75-125 g) dry pasta per person for a main course.

•Bring 16 cups (4 L) of water per pound (450 g) of pasta to a full rolling boil over high heat. Add 1 tbsp (15 mL) of salt and then the pasta.

•Stir until water returns to a boil. At this point, begin timing the pasta, and let cook, uncovered, at a full rolling boil, stirring occasionally.

•The only true way to tell if pasta is done is to try a piece. Use the times suggested on the package as a guideline. For pasta eaten hot with a sauce, it should be cooked 'al dente', or to the tooth. This means soft on the outside, with just a bit of resistance to the bite in the centre. For baked, layered or stuffed pastas, or for pasta salads, pasta should be cooked until it is almost soft through to the centre.

•When pasta has reached desired tenderness, drain, and serve immediately. Pasta should never be rinsed, unless it is for pasta salads, baked, layered or stuffed pastas, in which case it should be rinsed in cold water and drained to stop the cooking process.

•Cook pasta when the sauce it is to be served with is almost ready, so it can be tossed and served immediately. Stuffed and other layered, baked pasta dishes can be cut into pieces more easily if they are left to rest 10 minutes before cutting.

REHEATING PASTA:

•Microwave ovens reheat pasta very well. Simply cover the pasta and heat for approximately 1 minute on high power.

•Pasta can easily be reheated in a pot of boiling water. Submerge cooked pasta in rapidly boiling water for 30 seconds, drain and serve.

•Soups that contain pasta should be served immediately. If there are leftovers, the pasta will continue to absorb liquid; add additional stock or water to thin it out. Similarly, if you have stored leftover pasta salad in the refrigerator, add a bit of oil, vinegar, or another of the dressing's ingredients to re-moisten the salad.

PASTA NUTRITION GUIDELINES

Guidelines from Canada's Food Guide highlight pasta and other grain products as excellent food choices which contribute towards a healthy and well-balanced diet. Pasta is an excellent source of carbohydrates, vitamins and minerals. Canada's Food Guide suggests 5-12 servings of grain products per day, depending on personal activity levels. Be good to your body and include Primo pasta in your diet today!

THE PRIMO QUALITY COMMITMENT

Primo Foods Limited is committed to manufacturing only the highest quality pasta. Primo uses 100% Canadian durum wheat, a high-protein, low-starch wheat grown specifically for pasta because it delivers top-quality flavour, texture and a golden yellow colour.

PASTA SIZES, SHAPES AND SAUCES

One of the great things about pasta is its endless versatility and variety. Pasta shapes may be divided into five major categories:

SOUP PASTAS:
Soup cuts are available in a wide variety of interesting and unusual shapes. Soup pastas include shapes such as baby shells, stelline, acini di pepe, orzo and alphabet. Orzo is a great substitution for long grain rice as a side dish. Another great idea for soup, is to break up your favourite long thin pasta (capellini or vermicelli).

SHORT PASTAS:
Pasta cuts such as rotini, fusilli, penne, ziti, small shells and gnocchi are only a selection of the many cuts available in this category. Additionally, penne and pennine are available in two different varieties – lisce which has a smooth surface, and rigate which has a ridged surface. Short pastas are perfect for use in pasta salads, baked casseroles, and with thick and chunky sauces. The interesting grooves, ridges and twists of short pasta cuts capture and hold the chunky pieces in the sauces beautifully. Be creative and try some of the different Primo pasta cuts available.

LONG PASTAS:
Pastas in this category are either circular or flat and vary in thickness from very delicate and thin (capellini, vermicelli and spaghettini) to hearty and thick (spaghetti, fettucine and linguine). Long pastas are best suited for simple tomato sauces, oil-based sauces such as Pesto and cream sauces, which are smooth and thin, coating long pasta cuts evenly. Fish and clam sauces are often tossed with long pastas such as linguine, fettucine, and spaghetti.

NOODLES:
Primo's selection of noodle products contain real whole egg. Primo broad and medium egg noodles are traditionally served with heavy meat sauces but are well suited for casseroles and hearty soups. Egg noodles hold long-simmered sauces such as Bolognese and Beef Stroganoff very well.

SPECIALTY PASTAS:
Lasagne, jumbo shells, cannelloni, and manicotti are specialty pastas and are generally cooked, stuffed or layered with filling and baked with either cream and cheese or tomato sauces.

OVEN-READY OR REGULAR PASTA?
Primo oven-ready lasagne and cannelloni, which are made slightly thinner than traditional pastas, will lessen your time in the kitchen. The oven-ready pasta cooks in the recipe's sauce while in the oven, thereby eliminating the need to boil the noodles before baking.

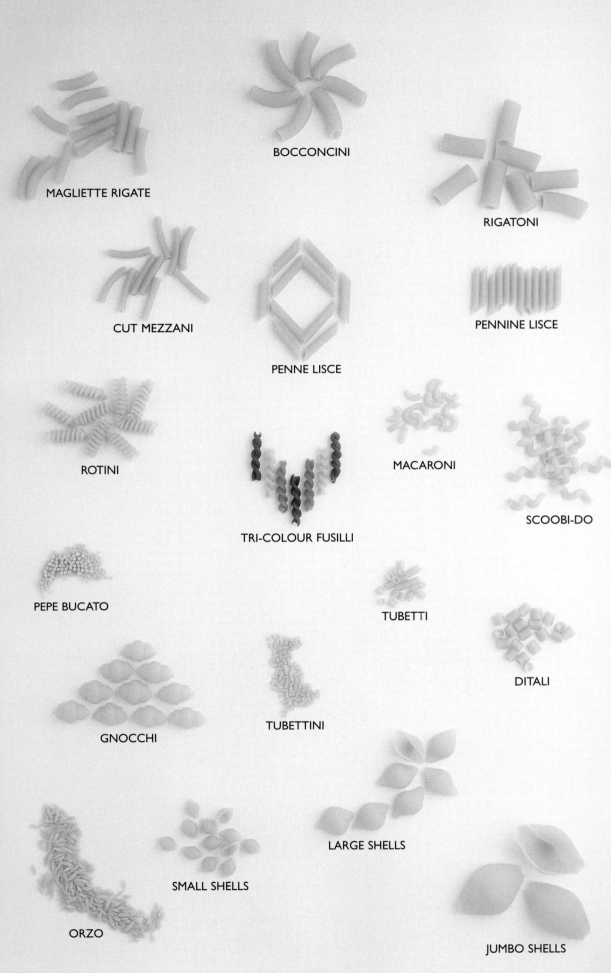

MAGLIETTE RIGATE

BOCCONCINI

RIGATONI

CUT MEZZANI

PENNE LISCE

PENNINE LISCE

ROTINI

TRI-COLOUR FUSILLI

MACARONI

SCOOBI-DO

PEPE BUCATO

TUBETTI

DITALI

GNOCCHI

TUBETTINI

LARGE SHELLS

ORZO

SMALL SHELLS

JUMBO SHELLS

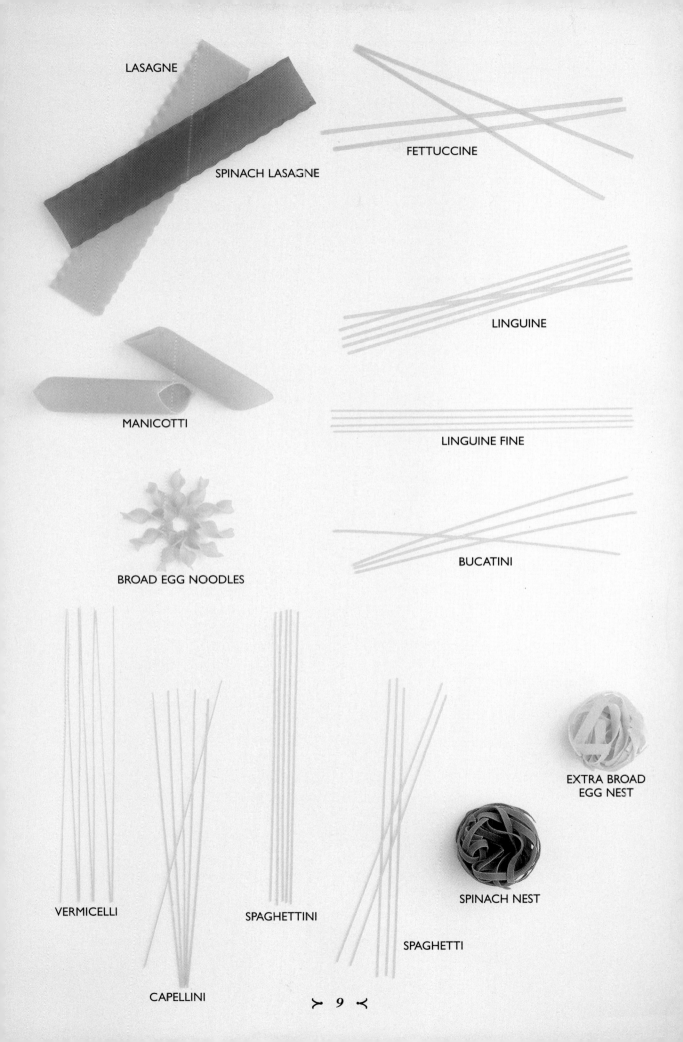

LASAGNE

SPINACH LASAGNE

FETTUCCINE

LINGUINE

MANICOTTI

LINGUINE FINE

BROAD EGG NOODLES

BUCATINI

VERMICELLI

SPAGHETTINI

EXTRA BROAD
EGG NEST

CAPELLINI

SPAGHETTI

SPINACH NEST

FRESH, WHOLESOME INGREDIENTS

We recommend you use only the freshest ingredients when cooking. We are sure that you will be pleased with the results! All of our recipes have been developed and tested using the following fresh ingredients:

FRESH GARLIC AND GINGER: To maximize flavour and freshness, we recommend using fresh garlic and ginger. Garlic should be stored at room temperature on the counter while fresh ginger is best stored uncovered in the crisper of your refrigerator. Buy fresh ginger and garlic in small amounts to ensure freshness. A 1-in (2.5-cm) square piece of ginger will yield approximately 1 tbsp (15 mL) finely chopped. Bottled, pre-chopped garlic and ginger are convenient alternatives.

LEMON AND LIME JUICE: Freshly-squeezed lime and lemon juices provide maximum flavour and freshness. If you don't have a juicer, stick a fork into the cut side of a lemon or lime half and twist. The juice of one medium lemon will yield approximately ¼ cup (50 mL) and the juice of one medium lime will give 2 tbsp (25 mL) juice.

HERBS

Recipes in this cookbook have been tested using fresh herbs where indicated to maximize the flavour and character of each dish. If you are unable to obtain fresh herbs from your grocery store, substitute ⅓ as much dried for fresh. Dried herbs have a stronger flavour than fresh. For example, if 1 tbsp (15 mL) of fresh thyme is called for in a recipe, use 1 tsp (5 mL) of dried thyme.

BAY LEAF: a dark green, long leathery leaf of the laurel tree; most often found dried – seldom available fresh.

BASIL: a sweet annual herb of the mint family with large, pale green rounded leaves; slight licorice flavour – ideal for flavouring soups and stews.

CORIANDER (CILANTRO OR CHINESE PARSLEY): a medium flat-leafed, green herb with a round leaf; distinctive peppery flavour; used often in Latin American, Mexican, and Asian cooking.

DILL: a feathery, dark green herb; used often in Scandinavian cooking, and for flavouring fish and seafood.

OREGANO: a green herb with medium-small rounded leaves; often used in Greek and Italian cooking.

PARSLEY: a fragrant annual or biennial herb available in curly and Italian flat-leafed varieties. The recipes in this book were tested using Italian flat-leafed parsley which is more flavourful. Curly parsley is perfect for garnishing.

ROSEMARY: a long, thin, needle-like herb with small leathery leaves; strong camphor flavour.

SAGE: an herb with large, long green leaves and a fuzzy appearance; subtle sweet taste, perfect for stuffings, breads, and vegetables.

THYME: a very small, round leafed herb; pungent taste — ideal for preparing stuffings, fish sauces, eggplant, mushrooms, and meat dishes.

FLAT LEAF ITALIAN
PARSLEY

OREGANO

ROSEMARY

CURLY PARSLEY

BASIL

DILL

THYME

CORIANDER

BAY LEAVES

SAGE

SPICES

Spices add that extra something to recipes that turn ordinary foods into interesting and aromatic meals. For extra flavour, buy whole spices and grind or crush just before adding to recipes. Whole spices will keep indefinitely while ground spices will begin to lose flavour after 1 year. Keep your spices in airtight containers away from direct heat and sunlight.

BLACK PEPPER: If you do not own a pepper mill, be sure to buy one — it is a kitchen must! Pre-ground pepper loses its flavour as soon as it is ground, so grind only as much as you will need.

CAYENNE: ground, dried, hot, red chilies; very hot.

CINNAMON: the bark of a tree; spicy, sweet, nutty flavour – cinnamon sticks can be used ground or whole for simmering in sauces.

CHILI POWDER: herb and spice mixture containing varying amounts of cumin, cayenne, and oregano.

CLOVES: intense, pungent, spicy flavour; can be used whole or ground.

CORIANDER SEED (WHOLE OR GROUND): used in Indian spice mixtures and European pastries.

CUMIN (SEED OR GROUND): a strong, earthy flavour; used in Mexican, Asian and Middle Eastern cooking.

FENNEL: a sweet annual herb with a subtle licorice flavour; grown for its flavourful seeds.

HOT PEPPER FLAKES: crushed dried hot red chilies; very hot.

NUTMEG: the seed of a tropical fruit; fragrant and sweet flavour. Buy whole nutmeg, and grate it as needed using the sharp, pointy side of a box grater or a nutmeg grater.

PAPRIKA: ground sweet peppers; sweet, mild flavour.

SAFFRON: the stigma of a variety of crocus; strong flowery flavour; gives simmered dishes a beautiful yellow colour.

TURMERIC: aromatic East Indian spice related to ginger; component of curry powders.

SOUP STOCK

The recipes in this book were tested using sodium-reduced, canned chicken and beef stock, and were diluted according to can instructions. Any unused portions should be refrigerated immediately in an airtight container and will keep for up to 3 days. If you use regular canned stock, you may find the end result too salty, so reduce any added salt accordingly. Powdered stock or stock cubes are extremely salty and often contain MSG; they are not recommended. When using homemade stock, season recipes with salt and pepper to taste.

CHILI POWDER

CAYENNE

PAPRIKA

TURMERIC

HOT PEPPER FLAKES

SAFFRON

CUMIN SEEDS

FENNEL SEEDS

CORIANDER SEEDS

CINNAMON

NUTMEG

CLOVES

Asian Influences

Naturally Brewed Soy Sauce: Look for a label that indicates naturally brewed — gives a more rounded flavour to your stir-fries; available in the Asian section of your supermarket. Refrigerate after opening.

Hoisin Sauce: A salty, soy tasting, thick, brown Chinese sauce, made from plum, soy, sesame and vinegar; available at most supermarkets; refrigerate once opened.

Oyster Sauce: A salty, slightly sweet, thick, brown sauce, made from oyster extract, flour and rice; available in most supermarkets; refrigerate once opened.

Sesame Oil: Made from pressed, roasted or unroasted sesame seeds; used as a flavouring, not as a cooking oil; refrigerate once opened.

Oriental Chili Sauce (Paste): Not to be confused with hot pepper sauce, Oriental chili sauce is thicker, and may contain ingredients such as plum, garlic and sweet potato, as well as chilies; hotness varies by brand; found in some supermarkets; refrigerate after opening.

Storing, Toasting and Using Nuts

Toasting nuts brings out their maximum flavour; we recommend toasting all nuts before using them in recipes. Watch carefully when toasting, nuts burn easily. If a recipe calls for toasted nuts and they are to be tossed together with a dressing or sauce, be sure to stir in the nuts just before serving, otherwise they will go soft and lose their crunchiness. Store all nuts in the freezer – they will keep fresh for many months. Never store nuts at room temperature — they will turn rancid, have a very bitter flavour and may be poisonous.

Almonds: Toast almonds in a 350°F (180°C) oven on a baking dish (a glass pie plate also works well) for 7 to 10 minutes, or until fragrant.

Pine Nuts: The easiest way to toast pine nuts is to place them in a small skillet over medium heat and stir for 3 to 5 minutes until they turn golden brown.

Pecans and Walnuts: Place nuts on a baking dish (a glass pie plate also works well) and bake for 5 to 10 minutes at 350°F (180°C), or until fragrant.

APPETIZERS AND HORS D'OEUVRES

Funghi Marinati

MARINATED MUSHROOMS

Mushrooms become very tender and juicy when marinated in this herb and lemon vinaigrette.

¼ cup	*each* **PRIMO 100% Pure Olive Oil, water and chopped fresh parsley**	50 mL
1	small onion, sliced	1
1	garlic clove, minced	1
1	bay leaf	1
½ tsp	*each* dried thyme and salt	2 mL
¼ tsp	pepper	1 mL
pinch	ground cloves	pinch
1 lb	small mushrooms	450 g

• In saucepan, stir together olive oil, water, parsley, onion, garlic, bay leaf, thyme, salt, pepper and cloves.

• Bring to a boil over medium-high heat; cook 2 minutes. Stir in mushrooms; cook 15 minutes over medium heat.

• Let cool in marinade and refrigerate. Serve at room temperature. Keeps up to 5 days in the refrigerator.

PREPARATION TIME: 10 MINUTES
COOKING TIME: 20 MINUTES
MAKES 2½ CUPS (625 mL)

Olive Marinate

MARINATED OLIVES

1	jar (375 mL) PRIMO Plain Queen Olives	1
¼ cup	*each* water, PRIMO Red Wine Vinegar and PRIMO 100% Pure Olive Oil	50 mL
½ tsp	*each* dried thyme, fennel and rosemary	2 mL
2	garlic cloves, crushed	2
2	bay leaves	2

• Drain olives and return to jar. Set aside.

• In small saucepan, stir together water, vinegar, olive oil, thyme, fennel, rosemary, garlic and bay leaves.

• Bring to a boil over medium-high heat; reduce heat and simmer 5 minutes. Pour vinegar mixture over olives; let stand at least 4 hours before serving. Keeps up to 3 weeks in the refrigerator.

GOAT CHEESE VARIATION: Combine ¼ lb (115 g) of goat cheese with 2 tbsp (25 mL) chopped fresh parsley. Using a tablespoon, form into 6 balls and roll in freshly ground pepper. Place in jar or container, and set aside. Cool vinegar mixture and pour over goat cheese. Marinate overnight.

PREPARATION TIME: 10 MINUTES
MARINATING TIME: 4 HOURS
COOKING TIME: 5 MINUTES
MAKES 1 JAR OF OLIVES

CROSTINI all'AGLIO
GARLIC CROSTINI

¼ cup	PRIMO 100% Pure Olive Oil	50 mL
2	garlic cloves, minced	2
1	baguette, cut into 1-in (2.5-cm) slices	1

● Preheat oven to 375°F (190°C). Combine oil and garlic in a small bowl.

● Place baguette slices on a baking sheet. Brush the tops of the slices with oil and garlic mixture. Bake 10 minutes or until lightly toasted. Serve with dips and spreads.

PREPARATION TIME: 5 MINUTES
BAKING TIME: 10 MINUTES
MAKES 32 CROSTINI

HOT ARTICHOKE DIP

A nice, hot dip to serve with crostini or pita crisps.

1	can (14 oz/398 mL) PRIMO Artichoke Hearts, drained and finely chopped	1
1½ cups	shredded low-fat mozzarella cheese	375 mL
1 cup	low-fat mayonnaise	250 mL
⅓ cup	PRIMO 100% Grated Parmesan Cheese	75 mL
2	garlic cloves, minced	2

● In bowl, stir together artichoke hearts, mozzarella cheese, mayonnaise, Parmesan and garlic until well combined.

● Spoon into a 4-cup (1 L), oven-proof dish. Bake at 350°F (180°C) for 25 minutes or until hot and bubbly. Can be made early in the day and baked just before serving.

PREPARATION TIME: 10 MINUTES
BAKING TIME: 25 MINUTES
MAKES 2½ CUPS (625 mL)

ROASTED RED PEPPER DIP

This super-fast dip can be spread on crackers or crostini, served as a dip for vegetable sticks, or piped into cherry tomatoes or snow peas.

1	pkg (250 g) light cream cheese	1
2	garlic cloves, minced	2
3	PRIMO Roasted Red Peppers, well drained	3

● Place cream cheese, garlic and red peppers in food processor; mix until smooth. Can be prepared 1 day before serving.

PREPARATION TIME: 5 MINUTES
MAKES 1½ CUPS (375 mL)

FOCACCIA

DOUGH:

1	pkg (8 g) dry yeast	1
pinch	granulated sugar	pinch
2 cups	lukewarm water	500 mL
4½ cups	all-purpose flour	1.125 L
¼ cup	PRIMO 100% Pure Olive Oil	50 mL
1 tsp	salt	5 mL
2 tbsp	PRIMO Cornmeal	25 mL

TOPPING:

3 tbsp	PRIMO 100% Pure Olive Oil	45 mL
2 cups	sliced onions	500 mL
½ tsp	salt	2 mL

———•———

● In a large bowl, dissolve yeast and sugar in ½ cup (125 mL) of lukewarm water. Let stand 10 minutes, or until frothy. Stir in remaining 1½ cups (375 mL) of lukewarm water and 2 cups (500 mL) of flour. Cover and set in a warm place for 45 minutes, or until frothy and almost doubled in volume.

● Using a wooden spoon, stir in 2 tbsp (25 mL) olive oil, salt, and another 2 cups (500 mL) flour. Turn out onto counter; knead for 15 minutes, adding flour as needed to prevent sticking. Dough should be smooth and elastic. Divide in two and form each half into a smooth ball.

● Coat bottom and sides of two 9-in (1.5 L) round cake pans with ½ tbsp (7.5 mL) olive oil each. Sprinkle each pan with 1 tbsp (15 mL) cornmeal.

● Place a ball of dough in each pan and press to edges. Cover both pans and place in a warm, draft-free place for 45 minutes, or until doubled in size. Poke dough all over with fingertips.

● Meanwhile, heat 1 tbsp (15 mL) olive oil in skillet. Add onions and cook 5 minutes, or until very soft and lightly browned. Set aside.

● Brush each pan of dough with 1 tbsp (15 mL) of olive oil and sprinkle with ¼ tsp (1 mL) salt. Divide and spread onion mixture evenly over both pans of dough. Bake at 450°F (230°C) for 20-30 minutes, or until lightly browned.

TIP: Combine Primo drained canned tomatoes with dried oregano, a pinch of salt and some olive oil for a tomato variation.

PREPARATION TIME: 30 MINUTES
RISING TIME: 1 HOUR, 30 MINUTES
BAKING TIME: 20 MINUTES
MAKES TWO 9-IN (23 CM) BREADS

Dissolve yeast and sugar in half of the lukewarm water. Let stand until frothy. Stir in remaining warm water and 2 cups (500 mL) of flour.

Stir in 2 tbsp (25 mL) of olive oil, salt and another 2 cups (500 mL) of flour.

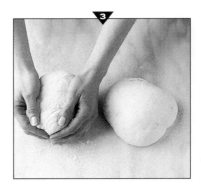

Knead for 15 minutes, adding flour as needed to prevent sticking. Dough should be smooth and elastic. Divide in two and form into two smooth balls.

Place each ball of dough in prepared pan and press to edges.

Cook onions in hot oil 5 minutes or until very soft and slightly browned.

Divide and spread onion mixture evenly over both pans of dough.

PITA CRISPS

*Pita crisps are perfect for dipping into Roasted Red Pepper Dip, Hummus,
Hot Artichoke Dip and Italian Bean Dip.*

2	pitas	2
⅓ cup	PRIMO 100% Pure Olive Oil	75 mL
2	garlic cloves, minced	2
¼ tsp	ground cumin	1 mL

● Preheat oven to 350°F (180°C).

● Place pitas on work surface and split in half to make 4 pita rounds.

● Whisk together oil, garlic and cumin. Brush rounds on both sides with oil mixture; cut each pita round into 12 wedges.

● Place pita wedges on baking sheet; bake for 20 minutes or until crisp and golden. Crisps keep up to 2 weeks in an airtight container.

PREPARATION TIME: 10 MINUTES
BAKING TIME: 20 MINUTES
MAKES 48 PITA CRISPS

CHICK-PEA HUMMUS

Be sure to use fresh lemon juice to enhance the flavour of this dip.

1	can (19 oz/540 mL) PRIMO Chick Peas, rinsed and drained	1
⅓ cup	PRIMO 100% Pure Olive Oil	75 mL
3 tbsp	lemon juice	45 mL
2	garlic cloves, minced	2
2 tbsp	tahini or unsweetened peanut butter	25 mL
½ tsp	salt	2 mL
	chopped fresh parsley	

● In food processor, combine chick-peas, olive oil, lemon juice, garlic, tahini and salt. Mix until smooth.

● Place in serving dish and garnish with parsley. Serve with pita crisps.

PREPARATION TIME: 10 MINUTES
MAKES APPROXIMATELY 2 CUPS (500 ML)

QUADRATINI di POLENTA GRATINATA con GORGONZOLA

GRILLED POLENTA SQUARES WITH GORGONZOLA

POLENTA:

7 cups	water	1.75 L
1 tsp	salt	5 mL
1½ cups	PRIMO Cornmeal	375 mL
¼ lb	Gorgonzola cheese, cut into 38 cubes	115 g
	PRIMO Vegetable Oil	

• In a heavy saucepan, bring water and salt to a boil over medium-high heat. Slowly add cornmeal in a thin steady stream, whisking constantly.

• Reduce heat to medium-low. Cook 20-25 minutes, or until thick and smooth, stirring constantly.

• Pour hot polenta onto a greased baking sheet (13¼ × 9¼ × ⅝ in) and smooth to edges. Cool until completely set.

• Oil and preheat grill. Turn cooled polenta onto a cutting board and cut into diamonds.

• Grill the polenta diamonds 2 minutes, or until lightly browned. Turn over and top each with a piece of cheese. Grill 2 more minutes or until cheese melts. Decorate with red pepper slices and basil leaves, if desired.

TIP: Cut cooled polenta into any shape using sharp cookie cutters.

PREPARATION TIME: 40 MINUTES
COOKING TIME: 30-35 MINUTES
GRILLING TIME: 5 MINUTES
MAKES 38 SQUARES

Slowly add cornmeal in a thin steady stream, whisking constantly to avoid lumps.

Pour hot polenta onto a greased baking pan and smooth to edges.

Turn cooled polenta onto cutting board and cut into diamonds.

Mini Pizzas

Create faces on mini pizzas as a treat for a child's party. Or, for a more sophisticated variation, top with any combination of pesto, sun-dried tomatoes, artichokes, fresh tomatoes, zucchini, peppers, chives, Brie or Camembert cheese.

1	pkg (6) English muffins	1
1	can (7.5 oz/213 mL) PRIMO Original Pizza Sauce	1
½ cup	sliced mushrooms	125 mL
2	green onions, sliced	2
1½ cups	shredded mozzarella cheese	375 mL

• Preheat oven to 400°F (200°C).

• Split each English muffin in half with fingers, and place split-side-up on baking sheet.

• Spoon 1 tbsp (15 mL) of pizza sauce on each half and spread to edges. Top with mushrooms, onions and cheese.

• Bake 15 minutes or until hot and bubbly. Pizzas can be prepared ahead of time and frozen. Bake frozen pizzas 5 minutes longer.

PREPARATION TIME: 10 MINUTES
BAKING TIME: 15-20 MINUTES
MAKES 12 MINI PIZZAS

ANTIPASTO

*Any type of salami will work wonderfully
in this appetizing hors d'oeuvre tray.*

1	jar (500 mL) PRIMO Giardinera Marinated Salad, drained	1
12	slices *each* Genoa salami, prosciutto and mild Provolone cheese	12
1	jar (170 mL) PRIMO Marinated Artichoke Hearts, drained	1
½ cup	*each* PRIMO Pitted Medium Ripe Olives and PRIMO Stuffed Green Olives, drained	125 mL
½ cup	*each* carrot and celery sticks	125 mL

● Place giardinera salad in the centre of a 12-in (30-cm) serving platter.

● Roll Genoa salami, prosciutto and Provolone into cylinders. Arrange attractively around salad.

● Arrange artichokes, black and green olives around salami and cheese. Finish tray with carrot and celery sticks.

TIP: Place carrot and celery sticks upright in a ½-cup (125-mL) dry measuring cup to measure.

PREPARATION TIME: 15 MINUTES
MAKES 8 SERVINGS

Cool rice mixture and stir in beaten egg yolk.

Divide and form rice mixture into 24 balls. Push one cube of mozzarella into each ball and form rice around it.

Panfry in batches until golden brown, approximately 45 seconds per side.

SUPPLÌ di RISO

RICE CROQUETTES

4 cups	chicken stock	1 L
2 tbsp	butter	25 mL
1⅔ cups	PRIMO Italian Style Arborio Rice	400 mL
⅓ cup	PRIMO 100% Grated Parmesan Cheese	75 mL
1	egg yolk, beaten	1
¼ lb	mozzarella cheese, cut into 24 cubes, ½-in (1-cm) each	115 g
2	eggs, beaten	2
1½ cups	PRIMO Italian Style Bread Crumbs	375 mL
	PRIMO Vegetable Oil	

—•—

• In saucepan, bring stock to a simmer. In heavy-bottomed saucepan, melt butter over medium heat; add rice and stir to coat.

• Gradually add chicken stock to rice, stirring constantly. Make sure each addition of stock is absorbed before adding the next. Stir in Parmesan and cool. Stir in beaten egg yolk.

• Divide and form rice mixture into 24 balls. Push 1 cube of mozzarella into each ball and form rice around it. Roll each ball in the beaten eggs and coat with bread crumbs.

• In deep skillet, heat several inches of vegetable oil over medium-high heat. Panfry the croquettes in batches until golden, approximately 45 seconds per side. Drain well on paper towel.

VARIATIONS: Stuff rice balls with diced ham, peas, and Provolone cheese, or with cooked, chopped chicken livers.

PREPARATION TIME: 5 MINUTES
COOKING TIME: 20-25 MINUTES
MAKES 24 CROQUETTES

GRILLED RATATOUILLE

Try cooking this wonderful mix of flavours under the broiler
for equally pleasing results.

½ cup	PRIMO 100% Pure Olive Oil	125 mL
¼ cup	PRIMO Red Wine Vinegar	50 mL
3	garlic cloves, minced	3
1	jar (313 mL) PRIMO Roasted Red Peppers, drained and quartered	1
½ cup	oil-packed sun-dried tomatoes, drained and coarsely chopped	125 mL
1	tomato, diced	1
1	eggplant, cut into ½-in (1-cm) slices	1
2	small zucchini, cut into ½-in (1-cm) slices	2
1	whole yellow pepper	1
1	red onion, cut into ½-in (1-cm) slices	1
½ lb	mushrooms, well cleaned	225 g
	salt and pepper	

• In small glass bowl, whisk together oil, vinegar and garlic. Set aside, reserving ⅓ cup (75 mL) for marinade. In large bowl, toss red peppers, tomato and sun-dried tomatoes together with remaining dressing.

• Preheat grill to medium-high. Grill eggplant and zucchini slices, 5 minutes per side or until golden brown. Brush with reserved marinade frequently. Remove from grill and add zucchini slices to tomato mixture. Cut eggplant into chunks and add to mixture.

• Place yellow pepper on grill; grill 5 minutes per side or until skin blackens. Place in small bowl and cover tightly with plastic wrap.

• Grill onion slices and mushrooms 10 minutes or until tender. Turn occasionally and brush with marinade. Remove mushrooms from grill and add to tomato mixture. Remove onion slices and chop coarsely; add to tomato mixture.

• Peel, seed and cube yellow pepper; add to tomato mixture.

• Gently toss all vegetables together, and let cool to room temperature. Season with salt and pepper to taste and serve with fresh bread.

PREPARATION TIME: 15 MINUTES
GRILLING TIME: 30 MINUTES
MAKES 8 CUPS

ITALIAN BEAN DIP

¼ cup	oil-packed sun-dried tomatoes, finely chopped	50 mL
2 tbsp	*each* PRIMO 100% Pure Olive Oil and lemon juice	25 mL
2 tbsp	chopped fresh basil or parsley	25 mL
2	garlic cloves, minced	2
¼ tsp	salt	1 mL
pinch	ground pepper	pinch
1	can (19 oz/540 mL) PRIMO White Kidney Beans, rinsed and drained	1

• Place sun-dried tomatoes, olive oil, lemon juice, basil, garlic, salt and pepper in bowl of food processor. Combine.

• Add beans; pulse on and off 10 times, or until mixture is chunky. Serve with pita crisps, crostini, or other bread.

PREPARATION TIME: 5 MINUTES
MAKES 1¾ CUPS (425 ML)

PASTA CHIPS

| 14 | PRIMO Lasagne Noodles PRIMO Vegetable Oil salt | 14 |

• Cook lasagne in boiling, salted water for 8-10 minutes, or until tender but firm. Do not overcook. Drain and rinse with cold water; drain again. Blot on paper towels.

• Toss cooked noodles with a bit of oil to prevent drying.

• Cut lasagne strips crosswise into quarters. Cut each square diagonally in half; each lasagne strip makes 8 triangles.

• In a deep, heavy pot, or deep fryer, heat oil to 350°F (180°C). Use a candy thermometer to measure the temperature of the frying oil. Fry pasta chips in batches for 90 seconds, or until golden.

• Drain on paper towels and season with salt. Serve with dips and spreads.

PREPARATION TIME: 15 MINUTES
FRYING TIME: 15-20 MINUTES
MAKES 112 CHIPS

BRUSCHETTA al POMODORO

TOMATO BRUSCHETTA

1	can (28 oz/796 mL) PRIMO Tomatoes, drained, seeded and chopped	1
¼ cup	PRIMO 100% Pure Olive Oil	50 mL
1	garlic clove, minced	1
1 tbsp	PRIMO 100% Grated Parmesan Cheese	15 mL
2 tbsp	chopped fresh basil (or 2 tsp (10 mL) dried)	25 mL
1	baguette, cut into ½-in (1-cm) slices	1
	salt and pepper to taste	

— Preheat broiler. In bowl, stir together tomatoes, olive oil, garlic, Parmesan and basil. Season to taste with salt and pepper.

— Place baguette slices on baking sheet. Broil 2 in (5 cm) from element for 45 seconds, or until browned. Turn over and toast other side. Remove from oven.

— Spoon 1 heaping teaspoon of tomato mixture onto each toast slice. Return to oven and broil 30 seconds, or until heated through. Serve warm.

TIP: The baguette slices may be toasted earlier in the day, but do not top the slices until ready to broil and serve.

WHITE BEAN VARIATION: Drain and rinse 1 can (19 oz/540 mL) PRIMO White Kidney Beans; place in bowl. Stir in 2 minced garlic cloves, ¼ cup (50 mL) PRIMO 100% Pure Olive Oil, ¼ cup (50 mL) chopped fresh basil or parsley, 2 tbsp (25 mL) PRIMO Red Wine Vinegar and 2 tbsp (25 mL) chopped PRIMO Roasted Red Peppers. Proceed as above for toasting and topping baguette slices.

PREPARATION TIME: 10 MINUTES
BROILING TIME: 5-7 MINUTES
MAKES 32 SLICES

In bowl, stir together tomatoes, olive oil, garlic, Parmesan and basil.

Broil baguette slices 45 seconds or until browned. Turn over and toast the other side.

Spoon tomato mixture onto toast slices. Broil 30 seconds or until heated through.

MEDITERRANEAN DIP

2 tbsp	PRIMO Vegetable Oil	25 mL
2	green peppers, chopped	2
2 cups	sliced fresh mushrooms	500 mL
1	can (7.5 oz) PRIMO Solid Light Tuna, drained and flaked	1
1	jar (313 mL) PRIMO Roasted Red Peppers, drained and thinly sliced	1
½ cup	*each* PRIMO Pitted Ripe Olives and PRIMO Stuffed Manzanilla Olives, sliced	125 mL
1	can (14 oz) PRIMO Tomato Sauce	1
½ cup	chili sauce	125 mL
½ cup	white vinegar	125 mL
2	bay leaves	2
pinch	ground cinnamon	pinch

● Heat oil in a saucepan over medium-high heat. Add green peppers and mushrooms; cook 3-5 minutes or until soft.

● Add tuna, roasted red peppers, olives, tomato sauce, chili sauce, vinegar, bay leaves and cinnamon. Bring to a boil over medium high heat.

● Reduce heat and simmer 15-20 minutes, or until vegetables are tender and sauce has thickened. Remove bay leaves, cool and refrigerate. Serve with crackers or breads. Keeps 1 week in the refrigerator.

PREPARATION TIME: 20 MINUTES
COOKING TIME: 20-25 MINUTES
MAKES 6 CUPS (1.5 L)

SUPER
SOUPS

VEGETARIAN PISTOU

*Pistou is the French version of pesto. It is traditionally made without nuts
and is a wonderful addition to this hearty soup.*

1 tbsp	PRIMO 100% Pure Olive Oil	15 mL
3	garlic cloves, minced	3
1	*each* onion and celery stalk, chopped	1
1	small zucchini, halved and sliced	1
¼ lb	green beans, cut into 1-in (2.5-cm) pieces	115 g
1	can (28 oz/540 mL) PRIMO Tomatoes	1
4 cups	vegetable or chicken stock	1 L
1 cup	PRIMO Tubetti	250 mL

PISTOU:

¼ cup	PRIMO 100% Pure Olive Oil	50 mL
½ cup	packed fresh basil leaves	125 mL
2 tbsp	PRIMO 100% Grated Parmesan Cheese	25 mL
2	garlic cloves, minced	2

● In large saucepan, heat 1 tbsp (15 mL) olive oil over medium heat. Add garlic, onion and celery, and cook 5 minutes or until tender.

● Stir in zucchini and green beans. Add tomatoes and break up with back of spoon. Pour in stock and bring to a boil. Add tubetti and cook 8 minutes, or until pasta and vegetables are tender.

● Meanwhile, combine remaining oil, basil and Parmesan in food processor; mix until smooth. Stir in garlic. Top each bowl of soup with 1 tsp (5 mL) basil pistou and serve.

PREPARATION TIME: 15 MINUTES
COOKING TIME: 15 MINUTES
MAKES 6 SERVINGS

Stracciatella

*This classic Italian soup is ideal on cold winter nights
when you're running late!*

8 cups	chicken stock	2 L
½ cup	PRIMO Orzo	125 mL
1	pkg (300 g) frozen chopped spinach, thawed, well-drained and finely chopped	1
1	egg, slightly beaten	1
¼ cup	PRIMO 100% Grated Parmesan Cheese	50 mL

• In large saucepan, bring stock to a boil over high heat. Stir in orzo; cook 10 minutes or until tender but firm.

• Stir in spinach. Pour beaten egg into boiling soup, stirring constantly. Sprinkle with Parmesan and serve immediately.

PREPARATION TIME: 5 MINUTES
COOKING TIME: 15 MINUTES
MAKES 4 SERVINGS

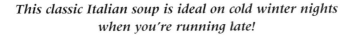

MINESTRONE

2 tbsp	PRIMO 100% Pure Olive Oil	25 mL
1	large onion, chopped	1
½ cup	*each* chopped celery, carrot and green pepper	125 mL
1	garlic clove, minced	1
5 cups	chicken stock	1.25 L
1	can (28 oz/796 mL) PRIMO Tomatoes	1
½ tsp	*each* salt and dried basil	2 mL
¼ tsp	*each* dried thyme and pepper	1 mL
1	bay leaf	1
1 cup	PRIMO Tubettini	250 mL
1	can (19 oz/540 mL) PRIMO Red Kidney Beans, rinsed and drained	1
2 cups	coarsely chopped fresh spinach	500 mL
2 tbsp	chopped fresh parsley	25 mL
	PRIMO 100% Grated Parmesan Cheese	

● In a large saucepan, heat olive oil over medium-high heat. Add onion, celery, carrot, green pepper and garlic. Cook 5 minutes or until vegetables are tender.

● Stir in stock, tomatoes, salt, basil, thyme, pepper and bay leaf. Bring to a boil. Reduce heat and simmer, uncovered, 10 minutes.

● Increase heat to high and bring soup to a boil. Add tubettini and cook 8-10 minutes, or until pasta is tender but firm.

● Stir in beans, spinach and parsley; remove bay leaf. Sprinkle with Parmesan and serve immediately.

PREPARATION TIME: 15 MINUTES
COOKING TIME: 25 MINUTES
MAKES 6 TO 8 SERVINGS

ZUPPA TOSCANA di FAGIOLI e PASTA

TUSCAN BEAN-PASTA SOUP

⅓ cup	PRIMO 100% Pure Olive Oil	75 mL
2	carrots, diced	2
3	garlic cloves, minced	3
4	onions, sliced into thick rings	4
6	celery stalks, diced	6
½ tsp	salt	2 mL
2 cups	thinly sliced Savoy cabbage or kale	500 mL
1	can (28 oz/796 mL) PRIMO Tomatoes	1
8 cups	chicken stock	2 L
2 tbsp	chopped fresh basil (or 2 tsp (10 mL) dried)	25 mL
½ cup	PRIMO Pepe Bucato	125 mL
1	can (19 oz/540 mL) PRIMO White Kidney Beans, rinsed and drained	1
12	thin slices Italian bread, toasted	12
⅓ cup	PRIMO 100% Grated Parmesan Cheese	75 mL
	freshly ground pepper	

● In large saucepan, heat 2 tbsp (25 mL) of olive oil over medium heat. Add carrots, garlic, onions, celery and salt. Cook 10 minutes or until onion rings are soft, stirring occasionally. Stir in cabbage and cook 3 minutes, or until cabbage slices wilt.

● Add tomatoes, stock and basil; bring to a boil. Add pasta and cook 10 minutes, or until pasta is tender but firm. Stir in beans and remove from heat.

● Preheat oven to 400°F (200°C). Place 4 slices of toast in the bottom of an oven-proof pot. Drizzle with 2 tsp (10 mL) of olive oil, sprinkle with 2 tbsp (25 mL) of Parmesan, and ladle with half of the soup. Repeat layers, and top with remaining toast, olive oil and Parmesan. Bake 10 minutes or until cheese is golden brown. Season with freshly ground pepper and serve.

TIP: You need an oven-proof saucepan or dutch oven for this soup. If you can't find Savoy cabbage or kale, use spinach.

PREPARATION TIME: 20 MINUTES
COOKING TIME: 25 MINUTES
BAKING TIME: 10 MINUTES
MAKES 8 TO 10 SERVINGS

Heat oil in a large saucepan. Add vegetables and salt, and cook over medium heat until onion rings are soft.

Bring tomatoes, stock and basil to a boil. Add pasta and cock until tender but firm.

Layer toast slices and soup in a oven-proof saucepan. Top with toast, olive oil and Parmesan.

CHICKEN RICE SOUP

1 tbsp	**PRIMO Vegetable Oil**	15 mL
1	**onion, chopped**	1
1 cup	**chopped carrots**	250 mL
¾ cup	**chopped celery**	175 mL
1 cup	**PRIMO Italian Style Arborio Rice**	250 mL
1	**can (28 oz/796 mL) PRIMO Tomatoes**	1
6 cups	**chicken stock**	1.5 L
1 tsp	**Worcestershire sauce**	5 mL
½ tsp	*each* **salt and hot pepper sauce**	2 mL
¼ tsp	*each* **dried basil, oregano and thyme**	1 mL
1	**whole chicken breast, cut into ¼-in (5-mm) cubes**	1

•In large saucepan, heat oil over medium heat. Add onion, carrots and celery; cook 5 minutes or until onion is soft. Add rice and stir until well-coated.

•Add tomatoes, stock, Worcestershire sauce, salt, hot pepper sauce, basil, oregano and thyme. Bring to a boil over medium-high heat.

•Reduce heat to medium-low; simmer uncovered for 20 minutes or until carrots are soft and rice is cooked. Stir in chicken; cook 2 minutes or until chicken is cooked through.

PREPARATION TIME: 15 MINUTES
COOKING TIME: 30 MINUTES
MAKES 8 TO 10 SERVINGS

CHICKEN NOODLE SOUP

*A super-fast, heart-warming soup, perfect to serve any evening
as a nutritious supper.*

1 tbsp	PRIMO Vegetable Oil	15 mL
2	green onions, chopped	2
1	*each* carrot and celery stalk, chopped	1
1	boneless chicken breast, cut into ½-in (1-cm) cubes	1
6 cups	chicken stock	1.5 L
1½ cups	PRIMO Medium Egg Noodles	375 mL
1 cup	frozen peas	250 mL
¼ cup	chopped fresh parsley	50 mL

• In large saucepan, heat oil over medium heat. Add onions, carrot and celery; cook 5 minutes or until slightly soft. Add chicken and cook 2 minutes, stirring constantly.

• Pour in stock and bring to a boil. Add egg noodles and cook 5-7 minutes, or until vegetables and noodles are tender. Stir in peas and parsley; cook until heated through. Season to taste with salt and pepper, and serve.

TIP: Use sodium-reduced canned chicken stock.

PREPARATION TIME: 15 MINUTES
COOKING TIME: 15 MINUTES
MAKES 6 SERVINGS

BLACK BEAN SOUP

2 tbsp	PRIMO Vegetable Oil	25 mL
2	garlic cloves, minced	2
1	*each* onion and carrot, peeled and chopped	1
1	celery stalk, chopped	1
1	bay leaf	1
½ tsp	*each* dried thyme, oregano and ground cumin	2 mL
¼ tsp	*each* salt and pepper	1 mL
3 cups	chicken stock	750 mL
2	cans (19 oz/540 mL) PRIMO Black Beans, rinsed and drained	2
1	can (14 oz/398 mL) PRIMO Tomato Sauce	1
¼ tsp	hot pepper sauce	1 mL
2 tsp	*each* lime juice and brown sugar	10 mL
	sour cream and chopped fresh parsley or coriander	

• In large heavy saucepan, heat oil over medium heat. Cook garlic, onion, carrot and celery 3 minutes, or until onion is soft.

• Stir in bay leaf, thyme, oregano, cumin, salt and pepper. Cook 30 seconds, stirring constantly. Pour in chicken stock and stir to combine; bring to a boil.

• Reduce heat to low, cover and cook 20 minutes, or until vegetables are tender. Discard bay leaf. Add black beans, tomato sauce, hot pepper sauce, lime juice and brown sugar to vegetable mixture.

• Place soup in blender, and purée in batches until smooth. Do not overfill blender. Return to saucepan and heat through. Ladle soup into warm bowls; garnish with sour cream and parsley, and serve.

PREPARATION TIME: 20 MINUTES
COOKING TIME: 45 MINUTES
MAKES 8 SERVINGS

ZUPPA di ZUCCA all'AMARETTO

AMARETTO SQUASH SOUP

An elegant first course soup that makes an interesting starter!

1 tbsp	**PRIMO Vegetable Oil**	15 mL
1	**900 g butternut squash, peeled, seeded and diced**	1
1	*each* **onion and potato, peeled and chopped**	1
3 cups	**milk**	750 mL
pinch	**nutmeg**	pinch
2 tbsp	**Amaretto (optional) salt and pepper**	25 mL
2	**PRIMO 'S' Biscuits, crushed**	2

● In heavy-bottomed saucepan, heat oil over medium heat. Cook squash, onion and potato 5 minutes or until onion is soft.

● Stir in 1½ cups (375 mL) of milk and bring to a boil. Do not worry, mixture will curdle. Reduce heat and simmer 7-10 minutes, or until vegetables are tender.

● Place soup in blender and purée in batches. Do not overfill blender. Return soup to pot. Stir in remaining milk, nutmeg and Amaretto, if using. Season with salt and pepper to taste.

● Gently re-heat soup; do not boil. Sprinkle crushed 'S' cookies on top and serve.

PREPARATION TIME: 10 MINUTES
COOKING TIME: 20 MINUTES
MAKES 6 SERVINGS

ZUPPA DI COZZE

MUSSEL SOUP

2 lbs	mussels	900 g
½ cup	white wine	125 mL
6	slices crusty bread	6
4	garlic cloves, minced	4
2 tbsp	PRIMO 100% Pure Olive Oil	25 mL
1	medium onion, chopped	1
1 tsp	dried basil	5 mL
1 tbsp	PRIMO Tomato Paste	15 mL
1½ cups	chicken stock	375 mL
1	can (28 oz/796 mL) PRIMO Tomatoes	1
2 tbsp	minced parsley	25 mL
	salt and pepper to taste	

— • —

• Rinse and scrub mussels; remove beards. Discard any with cracked or broken shells.

• In heavy-bottomed saucepan, bring wine to a boil over high heat. Add mussels and cover. Steam 90 seconds or until most of the mussels open. Discard any unopened mussels. Remove from heat.

• Using a slotted spoon, remove mussels from pot. Strain broth through a cheese-cloth-lined sieve and set aside. Toast the bread slices and rub one side with half of the minced garlic; set aside.

• In saucepan, heat olive oil over medium heat. Add onion, remaining garlic and basil; cook 3 minutes or until onion is soft.

• Stir in tomato paste and reserved broth. Increase heat to medium-high and cook 2 minutes, or until liquid is reduced by half. Add stock and tomatoes, breaking up tomatoes with back of wooden spoon. Bring to a simmer over medium-high heat. Season with salt and pepper to taste.

• Stir in mussels and heat through. Place 1 garlic toast in the bottom of each shallow soup bowl. Ladle soup into bowls and garnish with parsley. Serve immediately.

TIP: You can also prepare this recipe using small clams instead of mussels.

PREPARATION TIME: 15 MINUTES
COOKING TIME: 15 MINUTES
MAKES 6 SERVINGS

Rinse mussels and remove beards. Discard any with cracked or broken shells.

Bring wine to a boil over high heat. Add mussels and cover. Steam 90 seconds or until most of the mussels open.

Remove mussels from pot and strain broth through a cheese-cloth-lined sieve.

Add stock and tomatoes to onion mixture, breaking up tomatoes with back of wooden spoon. Bring to a simmer over medium-high heat.

Place 1 garlic toast in the bottom of each soup bowl. Ladle soup into bowls and garnish with parsley.

PASTA e FAGIOLI

PASTA AND BEAN SOUP

2 tbsp	PRIMO 100% Pure Olive Oil	25 mL
3	bacon strips, chopped	3
1 cup	*each* chopped carrot and celery	250 mL
1	onion, chopped	1
3	garlic cloves, minced	3
6 cups	chicken stock	1.5 L
1	can (19 oz/540 mL) PRIMO White Kidney Beans, rinsed, drained and mashed with potato masher	1
1	can (19 oz/540 mL) PRIMO Romano Beans, rinsed and drained	1
1½ cups	PRIMO Ditali Pasta	375 mL
	salt and pepper to taste	

• In large saucepan, heat olive oil over medium-high heat. Add bacon, carrot, celery, onion and garlic. Cook 7-10 minutes or until onions are lightly browned, stirring frequently.

• Stir in chicken stock, mashed kidney beans and romano beans. Bring to a boil over high heat. Add pasta and cook 8 minutes, or until pasta is tender but firm. Season to taste with salt and pepper.

TIP: You may use any small pasta in this soup: ditali, tubetti, tubettini, small shells or whatever you have on hand. For a smokier flavour, use Italian pancetta instead of bacon.

PREPARATION TIME: 15 MINUTES
COOKING TIME: 20 MINUTES
MAKES 6 SERVINGS

SPLENDID SALADS

INSALATA di FAGIOLI con TONNO

BEAN SALAD WITH TUNA

*An incredibly easy and satisfying salad that can be served with crusty
bread for a light lunch, or as a side dish to complete a meal.*

2	cans (7 oz/198 g) PRIMO Solid Light Tuna, drained and broken up	2
2	cans (19 oz/540 mL) PRIMO Romano Beans, rinsed and drained	2
1 cup	thinly sliced red onion	250 mL
3	Italian plum tomatoes, cut into wedges	3
1 cup	sliced PRIMO Pitted Medium Black Olives	250 mL
¼ cup	*each* lemon juice and finely chopped fresh sage and parsley	50 mL
2 tbsp	PRIMO 100% Pure Olive Oil	25 mL

• In a large bowl, combine tuna, beans, onion, tomatoes and olives.

• In a separate bowl, whisk together lemon juice. sage, parsley and oil. Pour over bean mixture. Toss to coat and serve.

PREPARATION TIME: 15 MINUTES
MAKES 8 SERVINGS

TOMATO-BASIL PASTA SALAD WITH GOAT CHEESE

6	Italian plum tomatoes, cut into quarters	6
⅔ cup	*each* PRIMO 100% Pure Olive Oil and thinly sliced fresh basil	150 mL
1¼ cups	crumbled goat cheese (about ⅓ lb/150 g)	300 mL
3	garlic cloves, minced	3
½ tsp	*each* salt and pepper	2 mL
1 lb	PRIMO Penne Rigate	450 g
1⅓ cups	shredded Asiago cheese	325 mL

• In a large bowl, combine tomatoes, olive oil, basil, goat cheese, garlic, salt and pepper. Set aside and marinate 2 hours at room temperature, or overnight in the refrigerator.

• In a large pot of boiling, salted water, cook pasta 11 minutes, or until tender but firm. Drain well.

• Toss hot pasta with marinated tomato mixture and Asiago cheese. Serve warm or at room temperature.

PREPARATION TIME: 15 MINUTES
MARINATING TIME: 2 HOURS OR OVERNIGHT
COOKING TIME: 11 MINUTES
MAKES 6 SERVINGS

THAI PASTA SHRIMP AND VEGETABLE SALAD

DRESSING:

⅓ cup	rice wine vinegar	75 mL
¼ cup	*each* PRIMO Vegetable Oil and chicken stock	50 mL
3 tbsp	soy sauce	45 mL
2 tbsp	peanut butter	25 mL
1 tbsp	minced fresh gingerroot	15 mL
1½ tsp	lime juice	7 mL
1 tsp	*each* sesame oil and Oriental chili paste	5 mL

SALAD:

20	snow peas	20
¾ lb	PRIMO Spaghettini	375 g
1	red bell pepper, sliced	1
4	green onions, chopped	4
½ cup	sliced water chestnuts	125 mL
12	baby corn cobs, cut into 1-in (2.5-cm) pieces	12
½ lb	cooked shrimp	225 g

• In food processor, combine vinegar, oil, stock, soy sauce, peanut butter, ginger, lime juice, sesame oil and chili paste. Process until smooth and set aside.

• In a large pot of boiling, salted water, blanch snow peas 60 seconds or until tender-crisp. Using a slotted spoon, remove from boiling water. Refresh in cold water, drain and set aside.

• In same pot of boiling, salted water, cook pasta 7 minutes, or until tender but firm. Rinse lightly, drain, and place in large bowl. Add snow peas, red bell pepper, green onions, water chestnuts, corn cobs and shrimp. Add dressing and toss to coat.

TIP: Look for chili paste and canned baby corn cobs in the Asian section of your grocery.

PREPARATION TIME: 20 MINUTES
COOKING TIME: 10 MINUTES
MAKES 4 SERVINGS

GREEK MEDLEY SALAD

*Serve this salad on Romaine leaves and you have a perfect
summertime side dish for grilled meat.*

1 cup	halved cherry tomatoes	250 mL
½ cup	*each* chopped English cucumber, sliced PRIMO Pitted Medium Ripe Olives and crumbled Feta cheese	125 mL
¼ cup	*each* chopped red and green onions	50 mL
2 tbsp	*each* PRIMO Red Wine Vinegar and lemon juice	25 mL
1	garlic clove, minced	1
⅓ cup	PRIMO 100% Pure Olive Oil	75 mL
¼ tsp	*each* dried oregano, salt and ground pepper	1 mL
2 cups	PRIMO Small Shell Pasta	500 mL
1 tbsp	chopped fresh parsley	15 mL

● In large bowl, toss together tomatoes, cucumber, olives, cheese, red and green onions. In separate bowl, whisk together vinegar, lemon juice, garlic, oil, oregano, salt and pepper.

● In large pot of boiling, salted water, cook pasta 9 minutes, or until tender but firm. Drain, rinse lightly and drain again. Place in bowl with vegetables.

● Drizzle with dressing and toss to coat. Garnish with parsley and serve.

PREPARATION TIME: 15 MINUTES
COOKING TIME: 8-10 MINUTES
MAKES 4 SERVINGS

GRILLED VEGETABLE PASTA SALAD

⅓ cup	**PRIMO 100% Pure Olive Oil**	75 mL
2 tsp	**salt**	10 mL
1 tsp	**pepper**	5 mL
1	**large eggplant, cut in ½-in (1-cm) slices**	1
2	**zucchini, cut in ½-in (1-cm) slices**	2
1	**large red onion, cut in ½-in (1-cm) slices**	1
3 cups	**PRIMO Penne Rigate**	750 mL
1	**garlic clove, minced**	1
⅓ cup	**PRIMO Red Wine Vinegar**	75 mL
2 tsp	**Dijon mustard**	10 mL
¼ cup	*each* **chopped fresh parsley and green onion**	50 mL
1	**jar (313 mL) PRIMO Roasted Red Peppers, drained and cut into strips**	1

● In small bowl, combine 2 tbsp (25 mL) olive oil, ½ tsp (2 mL) salt and pepper. Toss with eggplant, zucchini and red onion.

● Grill vegetables in batches over medium-high heat or broil 5 minutes per side until browned. Cut vegetables into chunks.

● Meanwhile, in large pot of boiling, salted water, cook pasta 8-10 minutes, or until tender but firm; drain.

● Whisk together remaining olive oil, salt and pepper with garlic, vinegar, mustard, parsley and green onion. In a large bowl, toss together pasta, grilled vegetables, roasted red peppers and dressing.

PREPARATION TIME: 10 MINUTES
COOKING TIME: 20 MINUTES
MAKES 6 SERVINGS

CAESAR PASTA SALAD WITH ROASTED GARLIC DRESSING

Roasted garlic imparts a sweet, subtle flavour to this salad.

1	head garlic	1
⅓ cup	PRIMO 100% Pure Olive Oil	75 mL
¼ cup	chicken stock	50 mL
2 tbsp	lemon juice	25 mL
1 tsp	*each* Dijon mustard and anchovy paste	5 mL
dash	hot pepper sauce	dash
4 cups	PRIMO Scoobi-doo	1 L
6	bacon strips, cooked and crumbled	6
1	small bunch Romaine lettuce, coarsely chopped	1
¼ cup	PRIMO 100% Grated Parmesan Cheese	50 mL

● Preheat oven to 300°F (150°C). Cut top off head of garlic and discard. Place garlic in centre of a square of foil and drizzle with 1 tbsp (15 mL) of olive oil. Bake 1 hour or until garlic is very tender.

● Meanwhile, whisk together remaining oil, stock, lemon juice, mustard, anchovy paste and hot pepper sauce; set aside.

● When garlic is cool enough to handle, squeeze softened cloves from skins into a small bowl. Mash with fork and whisk into dressing.

● In large pot of boiling, salted water, cook pasta 8-10 minutes, or until tender but firm. Drain and rinse lightly.

● In large bowl, toss together pasta, bacon, lettuce and cheese. Drizzle with dressing and toss to coat.

PREPARATION TIME: 20 MINUTES
BAKING TIME: 1 HOUR
COOKING TIME: 10 MINUTES
MAKES 6 SERVINGS

Place prepared head of garlic in centre of foil and drizzle with olive oil. Bake 1 hour until very tender.

Mash roasted garlic and whisk into dressing.

In large bowl, toss together pasta, bacon, lettuce and cheese. Drizzle with dressing and toss well to coat.

PENNINE ASPARAGUS SALAD WITH PARSLEY PESTO

*Using fresh Italian parsley for pesto is an excellent and
flavourful alternative to fresh basil.*

PESTO:

1 cup	packed fresh Italian parsley	250 mL
½ cup	PRIMO 100% Pure Olive Oil	125 mL
¼ cup	PRIMO 100% Grated Parmesan Cheese	50 mL
2 tbsp	toasted pine nuts	25 mL
2	garlic cloves, minced	2

SALAD:

1 lb	asparagus, cut into 2-in (5-cm) pieces	450 g
3 cups	PRIMO Pennine Lisce	750 mL
1	red bell pepper, cut into thin strips	1
½ cup	oil-packed sun-dried tomatoes, drained and cut into thin strips	125 mL
2	boneless chicken breasts, grilled and sliced (optional)	2

● Place parsley, olive oil, Parmesan and pine nuts in food processor; combine thoroughly. Stir in garlic and set aside.

● In large pot of boiling salted water, cook asparagus 2-3 minutes or until tender-crisp. Remove with a slotted spoon and refresh under cold water. Drain and set aside.

● In same pot of boiling water, cook pennine 8-10 minutes, or until tender but firm. Rinse lightly and drain.

● In large bowl, toss pasta with asparagus, red bell pepper, sun-dried tomatoes and chicken (if using). Gently stir in pesto and serve immediately.

TIP: The pesto for this salad can be prepared up to 2 days ahead of time. Toss with salad ingredients just before serving.

PREPARATION TIME: 15 MINUTES
COOKING TIME: 15 MINUTES
MAKES 6 SERVINGS

CURRIED CHICKEN PASTA SALAD

SALAD:

3	boneless chicken breasts	3
3 cups	PRIMO Gnocchi	750 mL
3	green onions, chopped	3
2	carrots, peeled and sliced	2
⅓ cup	raisins	75 mL
½ cup	toasted cashews or almonds	125 mL

DRESSING:

¾ cup	plain yogurt	175 mL
½ cup	low-fat mayonnaise	125 mL
2 tsp	curry powder	10 mL
1 tsp	liquid honey	5 mL
¾ tsp	salt	4 mL
½ tsp	pepper	2 mL
¼ tsp	dry mustard	1 mL

● Grill chicken breasts over medium-high heat 7 minutes per side or until cooked through. Remove from grill and cut into cubes.

● Meanwhile, in large pot of boiling, salted water, cook pasta 6-8 minutes, or until tender but firm. Rinse lightly and drain.

● In large bowl, combine pasta, chicken, onions, carrots and raisins.

● In a separate bowl, whisk together yogurt, mayonnaise, curry powder, honey, salt, pepper and dry mustard. Pour over pasta mixture and combine. Toss in cashews and serve immediately.

TIP: Prepare this salad up to 4 hours ahead of time, mixing in the cashews just before serving.

PREPARATION TIME: 20 MINUTES
COOKING TIME: 20 MINUTES
MAKES 6-8 SERVINGS

CURRIED WILD RICE, ORZO AND LENTIL SALAD

SALAD:

1 cup	wild rice, rinsed and drained	250 mL
1 cup	PRIMO Orzo	250 mL
1	can (19 oz/540 mL) PRIMO Lentils, rinsed and drained	1
2	celery stalks, sliced	2
⅓ cup	currants	75 mL
½ cup	almonds, toasted and coarsely chopped	125 mL

DRESSING:

2 tbsp	*each* white wine vinegar and apple cider vinegar	25 mL
1 tbsp	curry powder	15 mL
2 tsp	granulated sugar	10 mL
½ tsp	salt	2 mL
¼ tsp	*each* turmeric, ground coriander and ground cumin	1 mL
pinch	cayenne	pinch
¼ cup	PRIMO Vegetable Oil	50 mL

- In a large saucepan, bring 6 cups (1.5 L) water to a boil. Stir in wild rice and return to a boil. Reduce heat, cover and cook 40-45 minutes, or until tender but firm. Rinse lightly and drain.

- Meanwhile, in pot of boiling, salted water, cook orzo 10 minutes, or until tender but firm. Rinse lightly and drain.

- In large bowl, combine rice, orzo, lentils, celery and currants; set aside.

- In a separate bowl, whisk together white wine and apple cider vinegars, curry powder, sugar, salt, turmeric, coriander, cumin and cayenne. Gradually whisk in oil.

- Pour dressing over salad and toss lightly. Stir in almonds and serve.

PREPARATION TIME: 15 MINUTES
COOKING TIME: 45 MINUTES
MAKES 6 SERVINGS

NIÇOISE PASTA SALAD

SALAD:

4	potatoes	4
½ lb	green beans, ends removed	225 g
3 cups	PRIMO Rotini	750 mL
1	large tomato, cut into thin wedges	1
1	small red onion, thinly sliced	1
1 cup	PRIMO Pitted Black Olives, halved	250 mL
1	can (7 oz/198 mL) PRIMO Solid Light Tuna, drained and separated into large chunks	1
2	hard boiled eggs, cut into 4 wedges each	2

DRESSING:

¼ cup	*each* chopped fresh basil and PRIMO Red Wine Vinegar	50 mL
2	garlic cloves, minced	2
1 tbsp	Dijon mustard	15 mL
½ tsp	salt	2 mL
¼ tsp	pepper	1 mL
½ cup	PRIMO 100% Pure Olive Oil	125 mL

● In a pot of boiling, salted water, cook potatoes 20 minutes or until tender. Remove with slotted spoon and cut into cubes. In same pot of boiling water, cook green beans 2-3 minutes or until tender crisp. Drain, rinse under cold water and drain again.

● Meanwhile, in large pot of boiling, salted water, cook rotini 8 minutes, or until tender but firm. Drain and rinse lightly.

● In large bowl, toss together potatoes, green beans, rotini, tomato, onion, olives and tuna. In small bowl, whisk together basil, vinegar, garlic, mustard, salt and pepper. Slowly whisk in oil.

● Pour dressing over salad and toss gently to coat. Garnish with hard boiled egg wedges and serve.

TIP: To hard boil eggs, place eggs in a small saucepan and cover with cold water. Bring to a boil, remove from heat, cover, and let stand 18 minutes.

PREPARATION TIME: 25 MINUTES
COOKING TIME: 35 MINUTES
MAKES 8 SERVINGS

COLBY AND GOUDA PENNE SALAD

2 cups	broccoli florets	500 mL
4 cups	PRIMO Penne Rigate	1 L
½ cup	*each* cubed Gouda and orange Colby cheese	125 mL
½	red bell pepper, chopped	½
½ cup	*each* finely sliced red onion and PRIMO Medium Pitted Black Olives, sliced	125 mL
⅓ cup	bottled Italian salad dressing	75 mL

• In a large pot of boiling, salted water, cook broccoli 2-3 minutes or until tender-crisp. Remove with a slotted spoon, refresh under cold water and place in a large bowl.

• In same pot of boiling water, cook pasta 8-10 minutes, or until tender but firm. Drain pasta and add to broccoli.

• Stir in Gouda and Colby cheeses, red bell pepper, onion and olives. Drizzle with salad dressing. Toss to coat and serve immediately.

PREPARATION TIME: 15 MINUTES
COOKING TIME: 10-15 MINUTES
MAKES 6 SERVINGS

TURKEY WALDORF PASTA SALAD

An excellent way to use up leftover turkey from holiday dinners.

3 cups	PRIMO Bocconcini Pasta	750 mL
2 cups	cubed cooked turkey	500 mL
2	celery stalks, sliced diagonally	2
2	red-skinned apples, cored and cubed	2
¾ cup	low-fat mayonnaise	175 mL
¼ cup	low-fat yogurt	50 mL
1 tsp	Dijon mustard	5 mL
pinch	*each* salt and pepper	pinch
½ cup	toasted walnut pieces	125 mL
¼ cup	chopped fresh parsley	50 mL

• In a large pot of boiling, salted water, cook pasta 8-10 minutes. Rinse lightly, drain and set aside.

• Meanwhile, in a large bowl, toss together turkey, celery, apples, mayonnaise, yogurt, mustard, salt and pepper; combine well.

• Stir in pasta, walnuts and parsley. Serve immediately.

TIP: Be sure to use real mayonnaise for this recipe; other salad dressings are too strong.

PREPARATION TIME: 15 MINUTES
COOKING TIME: 15 MINUTES
MAKES 6-8 SERVINGS

TRI-COLOUR PASTA SALAD

DRESSING:

½ cup	*each* light sour cream and light mayonnaise	125 mL
3 tbsp	Dijon mustard	45 mL
1 tbsp	*each* sugar and lemon juice	15 mL
1	garlic clove, minced	1
½ tsp	*each* salt and pepper	2 mL

SALAD:

2 cups	*each* broccoli and cauliflower florets	500 mL
1	pkg (375 g) PRIMO Tri-Colour Fusilletti	1
3	green onions, chopped	3
1	small red bell pepper, chopped	1
1	carrot, chopped	1
¼ cup	chopped fresh parsley	50 mL

• In small bowl, whisk together sour cream, mayonnaise, mustard, sugar, lemon juice, garlic, salt and pepper; set aside.

• In large pot of boiling, salted water, cook broccoli and cauliflower 2-3 minutes or until tender-crisp. Remove with a slotted spoon, refresh under cold water and set aside.

• In same pot of boiling water, cook fusilletti 5-6 minutes, or until tender but firm. Rinse under cold water and drain.

• In a large bowl, toss together broccoli, cauliflower, fusilletti, green onions, red bell pepper, carrot and parsley. Pour dressing over salad and toss to coat.

TIP: Salad ingredients and dressing can be prepared up to 8 hours ahead of time. Toss salad with dressing just before serving.

PREPARATION TIME: 20 MINUTES
COOKING TIME: 10 MINUTES
MAKES 8 SERVINGS

BEEF, PORK AND POULTRY

BOCCONCINI WITH GRILLED CHICKEN, SUN-DRIED TOMATOES AND MUSHROOMS

This is a quick and easy summertime dish that tastes best with barbecue-grilled chicken.

1 lb	boneless chicken breasts	450 g
¼ tsp	*each* salt and pepper	1 mL
pinch	cayenne pepper	pinch
½ cup	oil-packed sun-dried tomatoes, cut into thin slices, reserving 1 tbsp (15 mL) oil	125 mL
4 oz	*each* fresh mushrooms and shiitake mushrooms	125 g
2	garlic cloves, minced	2
2	green onions, chopped	2
4 cups	PRIMO Bocconcini Pasta	1 L
1 tbsp	chopped fresh parsley	15 mL

• Trim fat from chicken breasts. Sprinkle both sides of each breast evenly with salt and pepper. Sprinkle cayenne pepper over one side of each breast.

• Grill each side over medium-high heat, 4-5 minutes or until juices run clear. Let stand 10 minutes; cut into slices and set aside.

• In skillet, heat sun-dried tomato oil over medium-high heat. Cook fresh and shiitake mushrooms and garlic 5 minutes, or until lightly golden.

• Stir in chicken, sun-dried tomatoes and green onions; cook 2 minutes.

• Meanwhile, in a large pot of boiling, salted water, cook pasta 8-10 minutes, or until tender but firm. Drain and toss with chicken mixture and parsley. Serve immediately.

PREPARATION TIME: 15 MINUTES
COOKING TIME: 20 MINUTES
MAKES 4 SERVINGS

BEEF STROGANOFF

1 lb	boneless sirloin steak	450 g
1 tbsp	PRIMO Vegetable Oil	15 mL
2 tbsp	butter	25 mL
1½ cups	sliced mushrooms	375 mL
1	onion, chopped	1
2 tbsp	all-purpose flour	25 mL
1½ cups	beef stock	375 mL
½ tsp	Worcestershire sauce	2 mL
1	pkg (375 g) PRIMO Medium Egg Noodles	1
½ cup	light sour cream	125 mL

• Cut steak into ¼-in (5-mm) strips. In skillet, heat oil and 1 tbsp (15 mL) of butter over medium-high heat. Add steak and cook 1 minute, or until browned, stirring frequently. Remove from pan.

• Melt remaining butter in pan and reduce heat to medium. Add mushrooms and onion; cook 3 minutes or until softened, stirring occasionally. Add flour and cook 1 minute, stirring constantly.

• Gradually stir in stock and Worcestershire sauce. Cook 3 minutes or until mixture begins to simmer, stirring constantly. Reduce heat to low and cook 10 minutes.

• Meanwhile, in pot of boiling, salted water, cook pasta 8-10 minutes, or until tender but firm. Drain pasta.

• Return beef to mushroom sauce and cook 2 minutes, or until meat is heated through. Remove from heat and stir in sour cream. Pour sauce over noodles and serve immediately.

PREPARATION TIME: 10 MINUTES
COOKING TIME: 20 MINUTES
MAKES 4 SERVINGS

TWO-MUSHROOM TOMATO PASTA TOSS

2	pkgs (10 g) dried porcini mushrooms	2
¼ cup	PRIMO 100% Pure Olive Oil	50 mL
1	onion, chopped	1
3	garlic cloves, minced	3
3 cups	sliced fresh mushrooms	750 mL
1	can (28 oz/796 mL) PRIMO Tomatoes, drained and chopped	1
½ cup	diced ham	125 mL
¼ tsp	salt	1 mL
4 cups	PRIMO Magliette Rigate	1 L
¼ cup	*each* chopped fresh parsley and PRIMO 100% Grated Parmesan Cheese	50 mL

● Soak dried mushrooms in 1 cup (250 mL) hot water for 30 minutes. Drain and slice mushrooms, reserving liquid. Strain liquid through a coffee filter and set aside.

● In large saucepan, heat oil over medium heat. Add onion and garlic; cook 3 minutes. Add fresh mushrooms and cook 2 minutes, stirring constantly. Add tomatoes, ham, salt and reserved liquid; bring to a boil. Reduce heat and cook 10 minutes.

● In large pot of boiling, salted water, cook pasta 8-12 minutes, or until tender but firm. Drain pasta.

● Stir porcini mushrooms into sauce and cook 2 minutes. Toss pasta with sauce. Sprinkle with parsley and Parmesan.

PREPARATION TIME: 20 MINUTES
COOKING TIME: 20 MINUTES
MAKES 4 SERVINGS

THAI-STYLE COCONUT CHICKEN STIR-FRY

This exotic dish has a delicate sweet taste.

SAUCE:

½ cup	coconut milk	125 mL
¼ cup	chicken stock	50 mL
1 tbsp	*each* soy sauce, lime juice and hoisin sauce	15 mL
1 tsp	Oriental chili paste	5 mL

STIR-FRY:

¾ lb	PRIMO Capellini	375 g
1 tbsp	*each* PRIMO Vegetable Oil and minced fresh gingerroot	15 mL
½ lb	boneless chicken breast, cut into cubes	225 g
1	green pepper, cut into squares	1
1	onion, cut into cubes	1
2 cups	sliced mushrooms	500 mL
½ cup	chopped fresh coriander	125 mL

● In small bowl, whisk together coconut milk, chicken stock, soy sauce, lime juice, hoisin sauce and chili paste; set aside.

● In a large pot of boiling, salted water, cook capellini 4 minutes, or until tender but firm. Drain, rinse lightly and set aside.

● In a wok, heat oil over medium-high heat. Add ginger and stir fry 15 seconds. Add chicken and stir-fry 90 seconds, or until just cooked. Remove chicken and ginger from wok, leaving as much oil as possible in wok.

● Add green pepper, onion and mushrooms to wok; stir-fry 2 minutes, or until pepper and onion are tender-crisp.

● Return ginger and chicken to wok; whisk and pour in sauce. Cook 30 seconds or until bubbly. Remove from heat; stir in coriander and pasta. Toss well and serve.

PREPARATION TIME: 15 MINUTES
COOKING TIME: 10 MINUTES
MAKES 4 SERVINGS

FAST AND EASY TURKEY STIR-FRY

1 cup	chicken stock	250 mL
2 tbsp	*each* cornstarch and soy sauce	25 mL
1 tbsp	lemon juice	15 mL
¾ lb	PRIMO Vermicelli	375 g
2 tbsp	PRIMO Vegetable Oil	25 mL
1	garlic clove, minced	1
1 tbsp	minced fresh gingerroot	15 mL
¾ lb	turkey breast, cut in thin strips	375 g
1 cup	halved snow peas	250 mL
1	green pepper, sliced	1
1	red onion, cut in chunks	1

• In small bowl, whisk together stock, cornstarch, soy sauce and lemon juice; set aside.

• In large pot of boiling, salted water, cook pasta 6-8 minutes, or until tender but firm. Drain and set aside.

• In wok, heat 1 tbsp (15 mL) of oil over medium-high heat. Add garlic and ginger, and stir-fry 15 seconds. Add turkey and stir-fry 2 minutes, or until turkey is cooked through. Remove from wok.

• Heat remaining oil in wok; add snow peas, green pepper and onion; stir-fry 2 minutes or until vegetables are tender-crisp.

• Return turkey to wok and pour in sauce. Cook 30 seconds, or until bubbly and heated through. Pour over pasta and serve immediately.

PREPARATION TIME: 10 MINUTES
COOKING TIME: 15 MINUTES
MAKES 4 SERVINGS

ROMANO CHEESE & BASIL PENNE WITH BEEF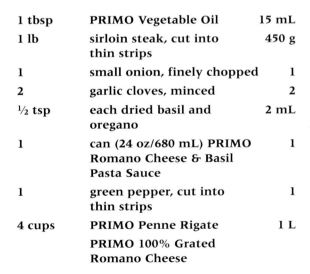

1 tbsp	PRIMO Vegetable Oil	15 mL
1 lb	sirloin steak, cut into thin strips	450 g
1	small onion, finely chopped	1
2	garlic cloves, minced	2
½ tsp	each dried basil and oregano	2 mL
1	can (24 oz/680 mL) PRIMO Romano Cheese & Basil Pasta Sauce	1
1	green pepper, cut into thin strips	1
4 cups	PRIMO Penne Rigate	1 L
	PRIMO 100% Grated Romano Cheese	

• In skillet, heat oil over medium-high heat; add beef and brown thoroughly. Stir in onion, garlic, basil and oregano.

• Reduce heat to medium and cook 3-5 minutes, or until onion softens. Stir in pasta sauce and simmer 10 minutes. Stir in green pepper and cook 5 minutes.

• Meanwhile, in a large pot of boiling, salted water, cook pasta 8-10 minutes, or until tender but firm. Drain pasta.

• Toss pasta with hot sauce until combined. Sprinkle with Romano cheese and serve immediately.

PREPARATION TIME: 10 MINUTES
COOKING TIME: 20 MINUTES
MAKES 4 SERVINGS

LINGUINE alla ROMANA

2 tbsp	butter	25 mL
¼ lb	ham, cut into thin strips	115 g
3	garlic cloves, minced	3
1	small red bell pepper, cut into thin strips	1
4 tsp	all-purpose flour	20 mL
1	can (385 mL) low-fat evaporated milk	1
½ cup	frozen green peas	125 mL
¾ lb	PRIMO Linguine Fine	375 g
	PRIMO 100% Grated Parmesan Cheese	

● In skillet, melt butter over medium heat. Add ham, garlic and red bell pepper; cook 5 minutes or until pepper is slightly softened.

● Sprinkle with flour and toss to combine. Stir in evaporated milk, making sure flour is thoroughly incorporated.

● Bring to a boil over medium heat, stirring occasionally. Cook 3-5 minutes or until thickened; stir in peas.

● Meanwhile, in a large pot of boiling, salted water, cook pasta 7 minutes, or until tender but firm. Drain pasta.

● Toss with hot sauce and Parmesan. Let stand 5 minutes before serving.

PREPARATION TIME: 10 MINUTES
COOKING TIME: 10 MINUTES
MAKES 4 SERVINGS

In bowl, whisk together pineapple juice, stock, soy sauce, vinegar, cornstarch and brown sugar; set aside.

In a small skillet, panfry prepared pasta mixture 5 minutes per side until golden.

Whisk the sauce and pour into wok; add pork and bok choy. Cook until sauce is thick and bubbly.

SWEET AND SOUR PORK STIR-FRY WITH NOODLE PANCAKES

SAUCE:

1	can (14 oz/398 mL) unsweetened pineapple bits, drain and reserve juice	1
½ cup	chicken stock	125 mL
¼ cup	*each* soy sauce, rice wine vinegar and cornstarch	50 mL
2 tbsp	brown sugar	25 mL

PANCAKES:

¾ lb	PRIMO Vermicelli	375 g
2	green onions, finely chopped	2
2	egg whites	2
1½ tsp	PRIMO Vegetable Oil	7 mL

STIR-FRY:

2 tbsp	PRIMO Vegetable Oil	25 mL
2	garlic cloves, minced	2
1 lb	pork tenderloin, cut in thin strips	450 g
1	onion, cut into chunks	1
1	red bell pepper, chopped	1
1 cup	*each* halved snow peas and chopped bok choy	250 mL

- In small bowl, whisk together pineapple juice, stock, soy sauce, rice wine vinegar, cornstarch and brown sugar; set aside.

- In a large pot of boiling, salted water, cook pasta 6-8 minutes, or until tender but firm. Rinse, drain and place in large bowl. Stir in green onions and egg whites.

- In a 6-in (15-cm) non-stick skillet, heat ¼ tsp (1 mL) of oil over medium heat. Spread 1 cup (250 mL) of pasta mixture to edges of pan. Fry 5 minutes or until golden brown. Turn and cook another 3 minutes, or until brown; remove from pan. Cook 5 more pancakes using remaining oil and pasta.

- In a wok, heat 1 tbsp (15 mL) of oil over high heat; add garlic and stir-fry 15 seconds. Add pork and stir-fry 2 minutes, or until browned; remove from wok and set aside.

- Pour remaining 1 tbsp (15 mL) of oil into wok. Add pineapple, onion, red bell pepper and snow peas. Stir-fry 2 minutes or until vegetables are tender-crisp.

- Whisk and pour sauce into wok; add pork and bok choy. Cook 1 minute, or until sauce is thick and bubbly. Top each pancake with sweet and sour pork and serve.

TIP: If you're in a hurry, you can omit the green onions and egg whites and simply serve the stir-fry over hot vermicelli.

PREPARATION TIME: 10 MINUTES
COOKING TIME: 1 HOUR
MAKES 6 SERVINGS

CHICKEN AND VEGETABLE PENNINE

1 tbsp	PRIMO 100% Pure Olive Oil	15 mL
¾ lb	boneless chicken breasts, sliced into thin strips	375 g
1	*each* red, yellow and green pepper, cut into thin strips	1
2 cups	quartered fresh mushrooms	500 mL
1	onion, chopped	1
2	garlic cloves, minced	2
¾ tsp	salt	4 mL
½ tsp	*each* pepper and dried basil	2 mL
3 tbsp	PRIMO Red Wine Vinegar	45 mL
4 cups	PRIMO Pennine Lisce	1 L
1	jar (6 oz/170 mL) PRIMO Marinated Artichoke Hearts, drained and sliced	1
½ cup	PRIMO 100% Grated Parmesan Cheese	125 mL

● In a non-stick skillet, heat oil over medium-high heat; add chicken and cook until browned. Remove from skillet.

● Add peppers, mushrooms, onion and garlic; cook 5-7 minutes or until peppers are tender-crisp. Stir in salt, pepper and basil; cook 1 minute. Return chicken to pan; add vinegar and toss to combine.

● Meanwhile, in a large pot of boiling, salted water, cook pasta 9 minutes, or until tender but firm. Drain and toss with chicken mixture.

● Add artichokes and Parmesan cheese to pasta mixture; toss to combine. Serve immediately.

PREPARATION TIME: 15 MINUTES
COOKING TIME: 15 MINUTES
MAKES 6 SERVINGS

SPAGHETTI alla CARBONARA

¾ lb	**PRIMO Spaghetti**	375 g
4	**bacon strips**	4
1	**egg**	1
¼ cup	**half-and-half cream (10% MF)**	50 mL
2 tbsp	**PRIMO 100% Grated Parmesan Cheese**	25 mL

• In a large pot of boiling, salted water, cook pasta 8-10 minutes or until tender but firm.

• Meanwhile, in skillet, cook bacon over medium heat for 5 minutes, or until crisp. Drain on paper towels, crumble and set aside.

• In a large bowl, whisk together egg and cream. Pour steaming hot drained pasta into cream mixture and toss well.

• Add crumbled bacon and Parmesan; toss well. Accompany with additional Parmesan and freshly ground black pepper. Serve immediately.

TIP: Make sure the pasta is steaming hot when tossed with cream mixture.

PREPARATION TIME: 5 MINUTES
COOKING TIME: 10 MINUTES
MAKES 4 SERVINGS

SPICY SAUSAGE AND GREENS PASTA

½ cup	**PRIMO 100% Pure Olive Oil**	125 mL
2	**leeks, white and pale green parts only, chopped**	2
¼ tsp	**salt**	1 mL
¾ lb	**hot Italian sausage, sliced**	375 g
½ cup	**chicken stock**	125 mL
½ tsp	**hot pepper flakes**	2 mL
6 cups	**coarsely chopped dandelion greens**	1.5 L
¾ lb	**PRIMO Rotini**	375 g
¼ cup	**PRIMO 100% Grated Parmesan Cheese**	50 mL

• In a large saucepan, heat olive oil over medium-low heat. Add leeks and salt, cover and cook 10 minutes, or until softened.

• Increase heat to medium; add sausage and cook 7 minutes, or until browned. Stir in chicken stock and hot pepper flakes. Add greens; cook 3 minutes or just until greens wilt, turning frequently.

• In a large pot of boiling, salted water, cook pasta 8-10 minutes, or until tender but firm; drain.

• Toss pasta with sausage and greens. Sprinkle with Parmesan and serve immediately.

TIP: Spinach or Swiss chard may be substituted for dandelion greens.

PREPARATION TIME: 15 MINUTES
COOKING TIME: 20 MINUTES
MAKES 4 SERVINGS

PASTA WITH STIR-FRIED BEEF AND VEGETABLES

STIR-FRY SAUCE:

⅔ cup	undiluted, canned beef broth	150 mL
2 tbsp	soy sauce	25 mL
1 tbsp	hoisin sauce	15 mL
1½ tsp	rice vinegar	7 mL
½ tsp	sesame oil	2 mL
2 tsp	cornstarch	10 mL

STIR-FRY:

1 tbsp	PRIMO Vegetable Oil	15 mL
1 tbsp	minced fresh gingerroot	15 mL
3	garlic cloves, minced	3
¾ lb	sirloin steak, cut into strips	375 g
1 cup	*each* onion, cut into strips, broccoli florets, quartered fresh mushrooms and whole snow peas	250 mL
1	red bell pepper, cut into cubes	1
¾ lb	PRIMO Capellini	375 g

- In small bowl, whisk together broth, soy sauce, hoisin sauce, vinegar and sesame oil. Sprinkle with cornstarch and whisk until lumps disappear; set aside.

- In a wok or large skillet, heat vegetable oil over medium-high heat. Cook ginger and garlic 30 seconds, stirring constantly.

- Add beef and stir-fry 3 minutes; remove ginger, garlic and beef; set aside. Add onion, broccoli, mushrooms, snow peas and red bell pepper; cook 5-7 minutes or until tender-crisp.

- Whisk and pour stir-fry sauce over vegetables; return beef, ginger and garlic to wok. Stir to combine. Bring to a boil and cook 3-5 minutes, or until sauce thickens.

- Meanwhile, in a large pot of boiling, salted water, cook pasta 5 minutes, or until tender but firm. Drain and toss with beef stir-fry. Serve immediately.

PREPARATION TIME: 25 MINUTES
COOKING TIME: 15 MINUTES
MAKES 4 SERVINGS

PENNE all'AMATRICIANA

1 tbsp	PRIMO Olive Oil	15 mL
1	¼-in (5-mm) thick slice pancetta, cut in thin strips	1
1	onion, chopped	1
3	garlic cloves, minced	3
½ tsp	hot pepper flakes	2 mL
¼ cup	white wine (optional)	50 mL
1	can (28 oz/796 mL) PRIMO Tomatoes	1
4 cups	PRIMO Penne Rigate	1 L
¼ cup	chopped fresh Italian parsley	50 mL
2 tbsp	PRIMO 100% Grated Parmesan Cheese	25 mL
1 tbsp	PRIMO 100% Grated Romano Cheese	15 mL

● In large skillet, heat oil over medium heat. Cook pancetta, onion and garlic 7-10 minutes, or until onion is very soft. Stir in hot pepper flakes and cook 1 minute. Pour wine (if using) over onion mixture, stirring to scrape up brown bits on bottom of skillet.

● Stir in tomatoes, breaking up with back of spoon; bring to a boil. Reduce heat to low and simmer 25-30 minutes, or until sauce thickens.

● Meanwhile, in a large pot of boiling, salted water, cook penne 9 minutes, or until tender but firm. Drain pasta.

● Toss immediately with tomato sauce, parsley, Parmesan and Romano cheeses, and serve.

PREPARATION TIME: 10 MINUTES
COOKING TIME: 40 MINUTES
MAKES 6 SERVINGS

FROM THE SEA

SHRIMP VEGETABLE STIR-FRY

SAUCE:

1 cup	unsweetened pineapple juice	250 mL
⅔ cup	oyster sauce	150 mL
2 tbsp	*each* soy sauce, rice wine vinegar and cornstarch	25 mL
2 tsp	sesame oil	10 mL
1 tsp	Oriental chili paste	5 mL

STIR-FRY:

¾ lb	PRIMO Linguine Fine	375 g
1 tbsp	*each* PRIMO Vegetable Oil and minced fresh gingerroot	15 mL
¾ lb	raw shrimp, peeled and deveined	375 g
1	onion, cubed	1
4 cups	broccoli florets	1 L
2	red bell peppers, cubed	2
½ cup	sliced water chestnuts	125 mL

● In small bowl, whisk together pineapple juice, oyster sauce, soy sauce, vinegar, cornstarch, sesame oil and chili paste; set aside.

● In a large pot of boiling, salted water, cook pasta 7 minutes, or until tender but firm. Drain, rinse lightly and drain again.

● In a wok, heat oil over medium-high heat. Stir-fry ginger 15 seconds. Add shrimp and stir-fry 2 minutes or until pink. Remove shrimp and ginger from wok, leaving as much oil as possible in wok; set aside.

● Add onion and broccoli; stir-fry 90 seconds. Add peppers and stir-fry 2 minutes, or until vegetables are tender-crisp.

● Return shrimp to wok and add water chestnuts. Whisk and stir in sauce. Cook 30 seconds or until sauce is bubbly. Remove wok from heat and add cooked pasta. Toss and serve immediately.

PREPARATION TIME: 20 MINUTES
COOKING TIME: 15 MINUTES
MAKES 4 SERVINGS

LINGUINE alle VONGOLE in SALSA ROSSA

LINGUINE WITH RED CLAM SAUCE

2 tbsp	PRIMO 100% Pure Olive Oil	25 mL
3	garlic cloves, minced	3
1	onion, chopped	1
1	can (28 oz/796 mL) PRIMO Ground Tomatoes	1
½ cup	dry white wine	125 mL
1 tsp	salt	5 mL
¼ tsp	pepper	1 mL
1	can (5 oz/142 g) PRIMO Baby Clams, drained, reserving liquid	1
1 lb	PRIMO Linguine	450 g
¼ cup	chopped fresh parsley	50 mL

- In large saucepan, heat oil over medium heat. Add garlic and onion; cook 3 minutes or until softened.

- Add tomatoes, wine, salt, pepper and ⅓ cup (75 mL) of reserved clam juice; bring to a boil. Reduce heat to low and simmer 10 minutes. Add clams and cook 5 minutes.

- Meanwhile, in a large pot of boiling, salted water, cook pasta 6 minutes, or until tender but firm. Drain pasta. Toss with sauce and parsley, and serve immediately.

PREPARATION TIME: 5 MINUTES
COOKING TIME: 20 MINUTES
MAKES 4 SERVINGS

SPAGHETTI al BACCALÀ

SPAGHETTI WITH SALT COD

This home-style Italian dish is perfect for fish lovers!

¼ lb	boneless salt cod (baccalà)	115 g
2 tbsp	PRIMO 100% Pure Olive Oil	25 mL
3	garlic cloves, minced	3
⅓ cup	chopped fresh parsley	75 mL
1	can (28 oz/796 mL) PRIMO Tomatoes, puréed	1
1 lb	PRIMO Spaghetti	450 g

• Place salt cod in a dish and cover with cold water. Place in refrigerator and let soak 24 hours. Change the soaking water several times.

• Cut cod into 1-in (2.5-cm) pieces. In saucepan, heat olive oil over medium heat; add garlic, parsley and cod. Cook 1 minute, stirring constantly.

• Add tomatoes and bring to a boil. Reduce heat to low and simmer 30 minutes.

• Meanwhile, in a pot of boiling, salted water, cook pasta 8-10 minutes, or until tender but firm. Drain well. Pour sauce over pasta and serve immediately.

SOAKING TIME: 24 HOURS
PREPARATION TIME: 10 MINUTES
COOKING TIME: 30 MINUTES
MAKES 6 SERVINGS

Soak salt cod in cold water for 24 hours, changing soaking water several times.

Cook garlic, parsley and cod in hot oil for 1 minute.

Add tomatoes and bring to a boil. Reduce heat and simmer 30 minutes.

CIOPPINO-STYLE LINGUINE

½ lb	*each* raw large shrimp and mussels	225 g
1 tbsp	PRIMO 100% Pure Olive Oil	15 mL
1	large onion, halved and sliced	1
4	garlic cloves, minced	4
1 tsp	*each* dried basil and oregano	5 mL
1	can (28 oz/596 mL) PRIMO Tomatoes	1
½ cup	dry white wine	125 mL
¾ lb	PRIMO Linguine	375 g

• Peel and devein shrimp; scrub, rinse and remove beards from mussels. Place shrimp and mussels in refrigerator, until needed.

• Heat oil in skillet over medium-low heat. Add onion and cook 7-10 minutes, or until golden brown. Stir in garlic, basil and oregano; cook 1 minute, stirring constantly.

• Add tomatoes and wine, breaking up tomatoes with wooden spoon. Bring to a boil over medium heat. Reduce heat and simmer 15-20 minutes, or until sauce thickens.

• Place mussels and shrimp on top of sauce, cover and cook 7-8 minutes, or until mussels open and shrimp turn pink. Discard any unopened mussels.

• Meanwhile, in a large pot of boiling, salted water, cook pasta 8-10 minutes, or until tender but firm. Drain, top with sauce and serve.

TIP: Scallops, lobster, clams, calamari or any other type of seafood complement this pasta entrée wonderfully.

PREPARATION TIME: 15 MINUTES
COOKING TIME: 40 MINUTES
MAKES 4 SERVINGS

CREAMY SEAFOOD LINGUINE WITH LEMON

2 tbsp	butter	25 mL
2	celery stalks, cut into matchstick-sized pieces	2
1	carrot, cut into matchstick-sized pieces	1
4	green onions, finely chopped	4
4 tsp	all-purpose flour	20 mL
2 cups	half-and-half cream (10% MF)	500 mL
¾ lb	cooked shrimp or scallops	375 g
2 tsp	finely grated lemon rind	10 mL
¼ tsp	salt	1 mL
pinch	pepper	pinch
¾ lb	PRIMO Linguine	375 g

• In shallow saucepan, melt butter over medium heat. Add celery, carrot and green onion; cook 5-7 minutes or until tender-crisp, stirring occasionally. Sprinkle evenly with flour and toss to combine. Cook 1 minute, stirring constantly.

• Stir in cream; bring to a boil over medium heat, stirring constantly. Reduce heat to medium-low and simmer 5 minutes. Add shrimp, lemon rind, salt and pepper; heat gently.

• Meanwhile, in a large pot of boiling, salted water, cook pasta 6-8 minutes, or until tender but firm. Drain well.

• Place linguine on serving plates and top with seafood sauce. Season with salt and pepper to taste and serve immediately.

PREPARATION TIME: 15 MINUTES
COOKING TIME: 15 MINUTES
MAKES 4 SERVINGS

FETTUCCINE WITH SMOKED SALMON AND ASPARAGUS

½ cup	butter	125 mL
2	garlic cloves, minced	2
2	green onions, finely chopped	2
1 tbsp	*each* chopped fresh dill and parsley	15 mL
4 tsp	fresh lemon juice	20 mL
1 lb	asparagus, cut into 2-in (5-cm) pieces	450 g
¾ lb	PRIMO Fettuccine	375 g
6 oz	smoked salmon, cut into strips	175 g

———•———

● In small skillet, melt butter over medium-low heat. Add garlic and cook 3-5 minutes, until fragrant but not brown. Stir in onions, dill, parsley and lemon juice; set aside.

● In large pot of boiling, salted water, cook asparagus 2 minutes or until tender-crisp. Remove with a slotted spoon and refresh under cold water. Drain and toss with 2 tbsp (25 mL) of herb butter; set aside.

● In same pot of boiling water, cook pasta 8-10 minutes, or until tender but firm. Drain and toss with remaining herb butter and asparagus.

● Place on serving platter. Gently toss in salmon and serve immediately.

PREPARATION TIME: 10 MINUTES
COOKING TIME: 20 MINUTES
MAKES 4 SERVINGS

PAD THAI

½ cup	chicken stock	125 mL
¼ cup	*each* oyster sauce and PRIMO Tomato Sauce	50 mL
2 tbsp	*each* sugar and fresh lime juice	25 mL
½ tsp	hot pepper flakes	2 mL
1	box (375 g) PRIMO Extra Broad Egg Nests	1
3 tbsp	PRIMO Vegetable Oil	45 mL
1	egg, slightly beaten	1
2	large garlic cloves, minced	2
1	red bell pepper, chopped	1
½ lb	raw shrimp, peeled and deveined	225 g
4 oz	boneless pork, cut into thin strips	125 g
2 cups	bean sprouts	500 mL
4	green onions, chopped	4
⅓ cup	chopped fresh coriander	75 mL
3 tbsp	chopped unsalted peanuts	45 mL

• In a small bowl, whisk together stock, oyster sauce, tomato sauce, sugar, lime juice and hot pepper flakes; set aside.

• In a large pot of boiling, salted water, cook pasta 6-8 minutes, or until tender but firm. Drain and set aside.

• In a wok or large skillet, heat 1 tbsp (15 mL) of oil. Add egg; cook 30 seconds or until set, stirring constantly. Remove from wok and set aside.

• Add 1 tbsp (15 mL) of oil to wok; cook garlic and red bell pepper 3-5 minutes, or until pepper is slightly softened. Remove and set aside.

• Heat remaining oil in wok; cook shrimp and pork 5-7 minutes or until shrimp turn pink.

• Stir in egg, peppers and pasta. Add bean sprouts and sauce; heat through. Spoon onto large serving platter and garnish with green onions, coriander and peanuts. Serve immediately.

TIP: Decrease the hot pepper flakes in this recipe to suit your taste.

PREPARATION TIME: 20 MINUTES
COOKING TIME: 25 MINUTES
MAKES 6-8 SERVINGS

In small bowl, whisk together stock, oyster sauce, tomato sauce, sugar, lime juice and hot pepper flakes; set aside.

Cook egg in hot oil for 30 seconds, or until set, stirring constantly. Remove and set aside.

Cook garlic and red bell pepper in hot oil until slightly softened. Remove and set aside.

Heat remaining oil; cook shrimp and pork 5-7 minutes, or until shrimp turns pink.

Return egg, peppers, and pasta to wok.

Stir in bean sprouts and sauce; heat through.

PASTA con TONNO e OLIVE

PASTA WITH TUNA AND OLIVES

*This quick pasta dish brings a Mediterranean flavour
to your family supper.*

2 tbsp	PRIMO 100% Pure Olive Oil	25 mL
2	garlic cloves, minced	2
1	can (28 oz/796 mL) PRIMO Tomatoes	1
½ tsp	*each* dried oregano, salt and pepper	2 mL
¼ tsp	hot pepper flakes	1 mL
1 lb	PRIMO Bucatini	450 g
1 cup	sliced PRIMO Medium Pitted Black Olives	250 mL
¼ cup	chopped fresh parsley	50 mL
2	cans (7 oz/199 mL) PRIMO Solid Light Tuna, drained and separated into pieces	2

● In saucepan, heat oil over medium heat. Add garlic and cook 10 seconds, or until golden brown.

● Add tomatoes, oregano, salt, pepper and hot pepper flakes; bring to a boil. Reduce heat to medium-low and cook 15 minutes.

● Meanwhile, in a pot of boiling, salted water, cook pasta 8-10 minutes, or until tender but firm. Drain well.

● Stir olives into sauce and cook 2 minutes. Toss pasta with sauce, parsley and tuna. Serve immediately.

PREPARATION TIME: 10 MINUTES
COOKING TIME: 20 MINUTES
MAKES 6 SERVINGS

Vegetable Favourites

PASTA PRIMAVERA

*Use whatever colourful fresh vegetables are in season
in this spring-time dish.*

8	asparagus spears, cut into 1-in (2.5-cm) pieces	8
1 tbsp	butter	15 mL
1	red bell pepper, seeded and cut into thin strips	1
1	*each* carrot and leek, cut into thin strips	1
4	garlic cloves, minced	4
1 cup	chicken stock	250 mL
2 tbsp	white wine or lemon juice	25 mL
¼ tsp	*each* salt and pepper	1 mL
1 cup	frozen green peas	250 mL
¾ lb	PRIMO Linguine Fine	375 g
¼ cup	*each* PRIMO 100% Grated Parmesan Cheese and chopped fresh Italian parsley	50 mL

• In a large pot of boiling, salted water, cook asparagus 2-3 minutes or until tender-crisp. Remove with a slotted spoon, refresh under cold water, drain and set aside.

• In skillet, melt butter over medium heat. Stir in red bell pepper, carrot, leek and garlic. Cook 5 minutes or until vegetables begin to soften, stirring occasionally.

• Pour in stock, wine, salt and pepper. Simmer 5-7 minutes or until vegetables are tender-crisp. Stir in peas and cooked asparagus.

• Meanwhile, in same pot of boiling, salted water, cook pasta 7-9 minutes, or until tender but firm. Drain and toss with hot sauce.

• Sprinkle with Parmesan and parsley; toss until well coated. Serve immediately.

PREPARATION TIME: 15 MINUTES
COOKING TIME: 15 MINUTES
MAKES 4 SERVINGS

HERBED PASTA AND CHICK-PEAS

1 tbsp	PRIMO 100% Pure Olive Oil	15 mL
1	garlic clove, minced	1
1	can (28 oz/796 mL) PRIMO Tomatoes	1
1 tsp	*each* dried basil and oregano	5 mL
½ tsp	pepper	2 mL
1	can (19 oz/540 mL) PRIMO Chick Peas, rinsed and drained	1
2 cups	*each* sliced fresh mushrooms and PRIMO Ditali	500 mL
¼ cup	chopped fresh parsley PRIMO 100% Grated Parmesan Cheese	50 mL

● In large saucepan, heat oil over medium heat. Add garlic and cook 30 seconds. Add tomatoes, basil, oregano and pepper, breaking up tomatoes with back of spoon.

● Stir in chick-peas; bring to a boil over high heat. Reduce heat to medium-low and simmer 10 minutes, or until sauce thickens.

● Meanwhile, in a non-stick skillet, cook mushrooms over medium-high heat for 3½ minutes, stirring often. Set aside.

● Meanwhile, in a pot of boiling, salted water, cook pasta 6-8 minutes, or until tender but firm. Drain well.

● Toss hot pasta with sauce. Top with mushrooms and sprinkle with parsley and Parmesan.

PREPARATION TIME: 5 MINUTES
COOKING TIME: 15 MINUTES
MAKES 4 SERVINGS

BOCCONCINI WITH ROASTED BELL PEPPERS AND MUSHROOMS

1	yellow bell pepper	1
1 tbsp	PRIMO 100% Pure Olive Oil	15 mL
1½ cups	sliced mushrooms	375 mL
1	onion, chopped	1
2	garlic cloves, minced	2
4	PRIMO Roasted Red Peppers, sliced	4
2 tbsp	white wine	25 mL
4 cups	PRIMO Bocconcini Pasta	1 L
2 tbsp	PRIMO 100% Grated Romano Cheese	25 mL
4	green onions, chopped	4

• Place yellow pepper on a baking sheet and broil each side 2-3 minutes, or until blackened. Place in a glass bowl and cover tightly with plastic wrap.

• When cool enough, peel blackened skin off pepper, seed and slice. Set aside.

• In skillet, heat olive oil over medium-high heat. Add mushrooms, onion and garlic; cook 5 minutes or until softened. Stir in roasted red and yellow peppers; add white wine and cook 3 minutes.

• Meanwhile, in a large pot of boiling, salted water, cook pasta 8-10 minutes, or until tender but firm. Drain pasta.

• Toss hot pasta with pepper sauce, cheese and green onions. Serve immediately.

PREPARATION TIME: 15 MINUTES
COOKING TIME: 10 MINUTES
MAKES 4 SERVINGS

Add rice to cooked onion and cook for 2 minutes, stirring constantly.

Add stock, ½ cup (125 mL) at a time, stirring constantly. Make sure each addition is absorbed before adding the next.

Remove from heat; stir in remaining butter and Parmesan.

RISOTTO ALLA MILANESE

SAFFRON RICE

7 cups	chicken stock	1.75 L
pinch	saffron threads	pinch
¼ cup	butter	50 mL
1	onion, finely chopped	1
2 cups	PRIMO Italian Superfino Arborio Rice	500 mL
¼ cup	PRIMO 100% Grated Parmesan Cheese	50 mL
	ground pepper to taste	

• In a saucepan, heat stock to steaming point. Add saffron and dissolve.

• In a heavy-bottomed saucepan, melt 2 tbsp (25 mL) butter over medium heat. Add onion and cook 3 minutes, or until softened. Add rice and cook 2 minutes, stirring constantly.

• Add ½ cup (125 mL) of stock, stirring constantly until all liquid is absorbed. Continue to add stock, ½ cup (125 mL) at a time, making sure each addition is absorbed before adding the next. Stir constantly. The rice should be slightly firm to the bite when done.

• Remove from heat; stir in remaining butter and Parmesan. Serve with freshly ground pepper.

TOMATO VARIATION: Omit the saffron. Follow the recipe above. When risotto is cooked, stir in ¼ cup (50 mL) chopped fresh basil, 1 large seeded and chopped tomato, and half a head of mashed roasted garlic (about 8 cloves). Add remaining 2 tbsp (25 mL) butter and Parmesan, and combine.

(To roast garlic, wrap 1 head of garlic in foil and bake at 350°F (180°C) for 1 hour. When cool enough to handle, break into individual cloves and squeeze pulp into a bowl).

MUSHROOM VARIATION: Omit the saffron and reduce stock to 6 cups (1.5 L). Soak two packages (10 g) of dried porcini mushrooms in 1 cup (250 mL) of hot water for 20 minutes. Remove softened mushrooms from water, chop and set aside. Strain mushroom soaking liquid through a coffee filter; add to 6 cups (1.5 L) of steaming stock. Follow the recipe above, using the mushroom liquid-stock mixture to cook the risotto. When risotto is ready, stir in sliced mushrooms, 2 tbsp (25 mL) of butter and Parmesan.

PREPARATION TIME: 10 MINUTES
COOKING TIME: 30 MINUTES
MAKES 4 TO 6 SERVINGS

LINGUINE al PESTO

LINGUINE WITH PESTO

2 cups	packed fresh basil leaves	500 mL
½ cup	PRIMO 100% Grated Parmesan Cheese	125 mL
¼ cup	pine nuts, toasted	50 mL
¾ tsp	salt	4 mL
¼ tsp	pepper	1 mL
½ cup	PRIMO 100% Pure Olive Oil	125 mL
4	garlic cloves, minced	4
1 lb	green beans, cut into 1-in (2.5-cm) pieces	450 g
1 lb	PRIMO Linguine	450 g

● Place basil, Parmesan, pine nuts, salt and pepper in food processor; mix until finely chopped. Slowly drizzle in oil with motor running; process until thoroughly combined. Stir in garlic and set aside.

● In a large pot of boiling, salted water, cook green beans 2-3 minutes or until tender-crisp. Remove with a slotted spoon, refresh under cold water, drain and set aside.

● In same pot of boiling, salted water, cook linguine 8-10 minutes or until tender but firm. Drain pasta. Toss with pesto and green beans, and serve.

TIP: Fresh Italian parsley may be substituted for basil in this recipe.

PREPARATION TIME: 15 MINUTES
COOKING TIME: 10-15 MINUTES
MAKES 6 SERVINGS

GARDEN TOMATO AND HERB SAUCE

2 tbsp	PRIMO 100% Pure Olive Oil	25 mL
2	onions, chopped	2
½ cup	*each* chopped celery and carrots	125 mL
1	small zucchini, chopped	1
2	garlic cloves, minced	2
1	can (28 oz/796 mL) PRIMO Whole Tomatoes	1
1 tsp	*each* salt, dried basil and oregano	5 mL
½ tsp	pepper	2 mL
2 tbsp	PRIMO Tomato Paste	25 mL
4 cups	PRIMO Bocconcini Pasta	1 L
	PRIMO 100% Grated Parmesan Cheese	

● In saucepan, heat olive oil over medium-high heat. Add onion, celery, carrots, zucchini and garlic; cook 5 minutes or until softened.

● Add tomatoes, salt, basil, oregano and pepper, stirring to break up tomatoes. Stir in tomato paste and bring to a boil. Reduce heat and simmer uncovered 15 minutes, or until sauce thickens.

● Meanwhile, in a large pot of boiling, salted water, cook pasta 9-10 minutes, or until tender but firm.

● Pour sauce over pasta. Sprinkle with Parmesan and serve.

PREPARATION TIME: 15 MINUTES
COOKING TIME: 20 MINUTES
MAKES 4-6 SERVINGS

SPAGHETTI WITH CAULIFLOWER

Cauliflower imparts a sweet flavour to this interesting dinner dish.

2 tbsp	PRIMO 100% Pure Olive Oil	25 mL
3	celery stalks, chopped	3
3	garlic cloves, minced	3
1	carrot, chopped	1
¼ cup	chopped fresh Italian parsley	50 mL
1	small cauliflower, broken into small florets	1
2 tbsp	PRIMO Tomato Paste	25 mL
pinch	hot pepper flakes	pinch
2 cups	chicken stock	500 mL
1 lb	PRIMO Spaghetti	450 g

- Heat oil in saucepan over medium heat. Add celery, garlic, carrot and parsley; cook 5 minutes or until vegetables soften. Add cauliflower, tomato paste and hot pepper flakes, stirring to coat well. Cook 5 minutes.

- Stir in half of broth, cover and cook 15 minutes. Add remaining broth and cook 15 minutes, or until cauliflower begins to fall apart.

- Meanwhile, in a large pot of boiling, salted water, cook pasta 8-10 minutes, or until tender but firm.

- Drain pasta and toss with cauliflower sauce. Top with freshly ground pepper and serve immediately.

PREPARATION TIME: 20 MINUTES
COOKING TIME: 40 MINUTES
MAKES 4-6 SERVINGS

Stir half the stock into cauli-flower mixture; cover and cook 15 minutes.

Add remaining broth and cook 15 minutes, or until cauliflower falls apart.

Drain pasta and toss with cauli-flower sauce.

SPAGHETTINI WITH SUN-DRIED TOMATO PESTO

Pesto takes on a new life using sun-dried tomatoes.

¾ lb	**PRIMO Spaghettini**	375 g
1 cup	oil-packed sun-dried tomatoes	250 mL
½ cup	chicken stock	125 mL
¼ cup	*each* **PRIMO 100% Grated Parmesan Cheese and PRIMO 100% Pure Olive Oil**	50 mL
2	garlic cloves, minced	2
2	green onions, finely chopped	2
⅓ cup	toasted pine nuts	75 mL

• In a large pot of boiling, salted water, cook pasta 6-8 minutes, or until tender but firm; drain.

• Place sun-dried tomatoes, stock, Parmesan, oil and garlic in food processor; mix until finely chopped and thoroughly combined.

• Toss together hot pasta, pesto and green onions until combined. Garnish with toasted pine nuts and serve.

PREPARATION TIME: 10 MINUTES
COOKING TIME: 8-10 MINUTES
MAKES 4 SERVINGS

EAST INDIAN CURRIED CHICK-PEAS

2 tbsp	PRIMO Vegetable Oil	25 mL
2	onions, finely chopped	2
2	garlic cloves, minced	2
2 tsp	minced fresh gingerroot	10 mL
1 tsp	curry powder	5 mL
1	can (28 oz/796 mL) PRIMO Tomatoes, drained and coarsely chopped	1
1	can (19 oz/540 mL) PRIMO Chick Peas, rinsed and drained	1
½ cup	water	125 mL
¼ tsp	*each* ground cinnamon and pepper	1 mL
¼ cup	chopped fresh mint or parsley	50 mL
1 tbsp	lemon juice	15 mL
1 tsp	finely chopped fresh green chilies	5 mL

● In large skillet, heat oil over medium-high heat. Add onions, garlic and ginger; cook 3-5 minutes, or until softened and lightly browned. Stir in curry powder and cook 1 minute, stirring constantly.

● Add tomatoes, chick-peas, water, cinnamon, pepper, mint, lemon juice and chilies. Stir to combine and simmer uncovered 10 minutes, or until thickened. Serve over Basmati rice or couscous.

PREPARATION TIME: 15 MINUTES
COOKING TIME: 15 MINUTES
MAKES 4 SERVINGS

PENNE all'ARRABBIATA

An authentic, spicy tomato sauce, suitable for all occasions.

2 tbsp	**PRIMO Olive Oil**	25 mL
1	**onion, finely chopped**	1
3	**garlic cloves, minced**	3
½ tsp	**hot pepper flakes**	2 mL
1	**can (28 oz/796 mL) PRIMO Italian Tomatoes**	1
2 tbsp	**PRIMO Tomato Paste**	25 mL
4 cups	**PRIMO Penne Rigate**	1 L
¼ cup	**coarsely chopped fresh parsley**	50 mL

⬤ In a shallow saucepan, heat oil over medium heat. Add onion; cook 5 minutes, or until soft and gold. Stir in garlic and hot pepper flakes; cook 2 minutes. Add tomatoes and tomato paste, stirring to combine.

⬤ Bring to a boil over medium heat. Reduce heat to low and simmer 30 minutes, or until sauce thickens.

⬤ Meanwhile, in a large pot of boiling, salted water, cook pasta 8-10 minutes, or until tender but firm.

⬤ Drain pasta and toss with tomato sauce and parsley. Serve immediately.

PREPARATION TIME: 10 MINUTES
COOKING TIME: 40 MINUTES
MAKES 4-6 SERVINGS

SPAGHETTI AGLIO e OLIO

SPAGHETTI WITH GARLIC AND OIL

This dish is an Italian classic that can be made in no time!

1 lb	**PRIMO Spaghetti**	450 g
⅓ cup	**PRIMO 100% Pure Olive Oil**	75 mL
4	**garlic cloves, minced**	4
¼ tsp	**hot pepper flakes**	1 mL
2 tbsp	**chopped fresh parsley**	25 mL
¼ tsp	**salt**	1 mL

⬤ In a pot of boiling, salted water, cook pasta 8-10 minutes, or until tender but firm.

⬤ Meanwhile, heat olive oil in a small skillet. Add garlic and hot pepper flakes; cook over medium-low heat 4 minutes, or until garlic turns pale gold. Remove from heat.

⬤ Drain pasta and toss with oil mixture, parsley and salt. Serve immediately.

TIP: Watch the garlic as it cooks, it can burn and turn bitter quickly.

PREPARATION TIME: 5 MINUTES
COOKING TIME: 15 MINUTES
MAKES 4 SERVINGS

LINGUINE alla PUTTANESCA

This classic sauce hails from Rome.

1	can (28 oz/796 mL) PRIMO Tomatoes	1
2 tbsp	PRIMO 100% Pure Olive Oil	25 mL
2	canned anchovy filets, drained and finely chopped (optional)	2
4	garlic cloves, minced	4
½ cup	*each* sliced PRIMO Pitted Medium Ripe Olives and sliced PRIMO Stuffed Manzanilla Olives	125 mL
2 tbsp	drained capers	25 mL
½ tsp	hot pepper flakes	2 mL
¼ tsp	*each* dried oregano and salt	1 mL
¾ lb	PRIMO Linguine	375 g
¼ cup	chopped fresh Italian parsley	50 mL

• Place tomatoes and juice in food processor. Pulse on and off until tomatoes are crushed; set aside.

• In large skillet, heat olive oil over medium heat. Add anchovies (if using), garlic, olives, capers, hot pepper flakes, oregano and salt. Cook 3 minutes or until garlic softens, stirring constantly. Stir in tomatoes; cook 20 minutes or until sauce thickens.

• Meanwhile, in a pot of boiling, salted water, cook pasta 6 minutes, or until tender but firm. Drain well. Toss with sauce and fresh parsley. Serve immediately.

PREPARATION TIME: 10 MINUTES
COOKING TIME: 25 MINUTES
MAKES 4 SERVINGS

LINGUINE WITH CARAMELIZED ONIONS

¼ cup	PRIMO Olive Oil	50 mL
2	large onions, sliced	2
1 tsp	granulated sugar	5 mL
2	Italian plum tomatoes, finely chopped	2
2 tbsp	chopped fresh basil	25 mL
¾ cup	chicken stock	175 mL
¾ lb	PRIMO Linguine Fine	375 g
	salt and pepper to taste	

• In a skillet, heat 2 tbsp (25 mL) of oil over medium-low heat. Add onions and sprinkle with sugar; cook slowly 20-25 minutes or until onions are very soft and caramel-coloured. Decrease heat to low if onions burn before they caramelize.

• Stir in tomatoes, basil and chicken stock; heat through.

• Meanwhile, in a large pot of boiling, salted water, cook pasta 8-10 minutes, or until tender but firm.

• Drain pasta and toss with onion mixture. Season with salt and pepper to taste. Serve with a dry white wine and soft bread.

PREPARATION TIME: 10 MINUTES
COOKING TIME: 30 MINUTES
MAKES 4 SERVINGS

ROTINI WITH SWISS CHARD, PINE NUTS AND RAISINS

4 cups	PRIMO Rotini	1 L
2 tbsp	PRIMO 100% Pure Olive Oil	25 mL
4	green onions, chopped	4
½ tsp	*each* salt and pepper	2 mL
4 cups	shredded Swiss chard	1 L
⅓ cup	raisins	75 mL
1 tbsp	PRIMO Red Wine Vinegar	15 mL
¼ cup	toasted pine nuts	50 mL

●In a large pot of boiling, salted water, cook pasta 8-10 minutes, or until tender but firm.

●Meanwhile, heat oil in skillet over medium heat. Add onions and cook 3 minutes, or until softened. Season with salt and pepper; stir to combine.

●Stir in Swiss chard, raisins and vinegar. Cook 2-3 minutes or until Swiss chard begins to wilt, but remains bright green.

●Drain pasta; toss with Swiss chard and pine nuts until well-combined. Serve immediately.

PREPARATION TIME: 10 MINUTES
COOKING TIME: 10 MINUTES
MAKES 4 SERVINGS

SPAGHETTINI WITH EGGPLANT AND TOMATO

1 lb	eggplant	450 g
2 tsp	salt	10 mL
2 tbsp	PRIMO Vegetable Oil	25 mL
2	garlic cloves, minced	2
1	can (28 oz/796 mL) PRIMO Tomatoes	1
½ tsp	hot pepper flakes	2 mL
1 lb	PRIMO Spaghettini	450 g
2 tbsp	chopped fresh parsley	25 mL

• Slice eggplant lengthwise into ¼-in (5-mm) slices. Cut each slice lengthwise into ¼-in (5 mm) strips.

• Toss strips with salt and place in colander to drain. Let stand 30 minutes and press out liquid. Rinse, drain and pat dry.

• Heat oil in skillet over medium heat. Add eggplant strips and garlic; cook 5 minutes or until softened.

• Add tomatoes and hot pepper flakes; bring to a boil. Reduce heat to medium-low and simmer 10 minutes, or until eggplant is tender but not mushy.

• Meanwhile, in a pot of boiling, salted water, cook pasta 7 minutes, or until tender but firm. Drain and toss pasta with tomato-eggplant sauce. Garnish with parsley and serve.

PREPARATION TIME: 15 MINUTES
DRAINING TIME: 30 MINUTES
COOKING TIME: 15 MINUTES
MAKES 6 SERVINGS

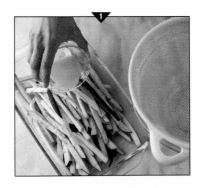

Toss eggplant strips with salt and place in colander to drain, pressing out liquid.

Rinse eggplant strips, drain and pat dry.

Add tomatoes and hot pepper flakes to cooked eggplant mixture; simmer 10 minutes until eggplant is tender.

POLENTA

Serve polenta with any stewed or braised meat that has lots of gravy.

7 cups	**water**	**1.75 L**
1 tsp	**salt**	**5 mL**
1½ cups	**PRIMO Cornmeal**	**375 mL**

—•—

• In a heavy, non-aluminum saucepan, bring water and salt to a boil over medium-high heat. Add the cornmeal in a thin steady stream, whisking constantly.

• When all the cornmeal has been added, reduce heat to medium-low and whisk constantly for 20-25 minutes. As the polenta thickens, stir with a wooden spoon.

VARIATION: Try cooling polenta on a baking sheet, cutting into "french fries" and pan-frying until golden. Sprinkle with extra Parmesan and serve. For a different taste, stir butter and Parmesan into polenta.

PREPARATION TIME: 5 MINUTES
COOKING TIME: 35 MINUTES
MAKES 4 CUPS

CREAMY
CREATIONS

FETTUCCINE ALFREDO

*This classic dish hails from northern Italy
and takes just minutes to prepare.*

1 lb	**PRIMO Fettuccine**	450 g
½ cup	table cream (18% MF)	125 mL
¼ cup	butter	50 mL
½ cup	**PRIMO 100% Grated Parmesan Cheese**	125 mL
pinch	nutmeg	pinch

● In a pot of boiling, salted water, cook pasta 7 minutes, or until tender but firm. Drain well.

● Meanwhile, in saucepan, heat cream and butter over medium-low heat 1 minute, or until butter melts.

● Add drained pasta and combine thoroughly. Sprinkle with Parmesan and toss. Sprinkle with nutmeg and serve immediately.

PREPARATION TIME: 5 MINUTES
COOKING TIME: 10 MINUTES
MAKES 4 SERVINGS

LIGHT FETTUCCINE ALFREDO

A simply superb, rich-tasting alternative to a classic Alfredo.

1 cup	**light ricotta cheese**	250 mL
½ cup	*each* **PRIMO 100% Grated Parmesan Cheese and milk**	125 mL
¾ tsp	**freshly ground pepper**	4 mL
½ tsp	**salt**	2 mL
1 lb	**PRIMO Fettuccine**	450 g

● Place ricotta, Parmesan, milk, pepper and salt in blender. Purée until smooth and set aside.

● In a large pot of boiling, salted water, cook pasta 8-10 minutes, or until tender but firm. Drain and return to pot; add ricotta cheese mixture. Toss together until pasta is hot and creamy.

PREPARATION TIME: 5 MINUTES
COOKING TIME: 10 MINUTES
MAKES 6 SERVINGS

FETTUCCINE ALFREDO

Pasta ai QUATTRO FORMAGGI

PASTA WITH FOUR CHEESES

Serve this pasta dish with a salad to make a quick, delicious meal.

1 lb	**PRIMO Cut Mezzani**	450 g
¼ cup	*each* **butter and half-and-half cream**	50 mL
¼ cup	*each* **PRIMO 100% Grated Parmesan Cheese and crumbled Gorgonzola cheese**	50 mL
½ cup	*each* **shredded Provolone and Fontina cheese**	125 mL
½ tsp	**pepper**	2 mL

• In a large pot of boiling, salted water, cook pasta 8-10 minutes, or until tender but firm. Drain and set aside.

• In same pot, melt butter over low heat. Add cream and drained pasta; combine thoroughly.

• Add Parmesan, Gorgonzola, Provolone and Fontina cheeses one at a time, stirring constantly. Cook until cheeses melt, stirring constantly.

• Stir in pepper and serve immediately.

TIP: Use any cheeses you have on hand, but make sure to include Parmesan and at least one strong cheese.

PREPARATION TIME: 5 MINUTES
COOKING TIME: 15 MINUTES
MAKES 4 SERVINGS

CREAMY TOMATO VODKA SAUCE

Serve this indulgent pasta dish as a main course, or as a side dish to a light meal.

1 tbsp	**PRIMO 100% Pure Olive Oil**	15 mL
3	**garlic cloves, minced**	3
1	**small onion, finely chopped**	1
2	**bacon strips, finely chopped**	2
1½ cups	**whipping cream**	375 mL
¼ cup	**vodka**	50 mL
½ tsp	*each* **salt and pepper**	2 mL
1	**can (5.5 oz/156 mL) PRIMO Tomato Paste**	1
4 cups	**PRIMO Penne Rigate**	1 L
¼ cup	**PRIMO 100% Grated Parmesan Cheese**	50 mL

• Heat oil in saucepan over medium heat. Stir in garlic, onion and bacon; cook 5-7 minutes or until lightly browned.

• Stir in cream, vodka, salt, pepper and tomato paste. Reduce heat and simmer 10 minutes.

• Meanwhile, in a large pot of boiling, salted water, cook pasta 11 minutes, or until tender but firm.

• Stir 2 tbsp (25 mL) Parmesan into tomato sauce. Add pasta and toss to coat. Sprinkle with remaining Parmesan and serve.

PREPARATION TIME: 10 MINUTES
COOKING TIME: 20 MINUTES
MAKES 6 SERVINGS

SPAGHETTI alla MOZZARELLA

MOZZARELLA SPAGHETTI

Be sure to use only garden-fresh tomatoes and basil – nothing else will do!

3	tomatoes, cut into cubes	3
1½ cups	cubed mozzarella cheese	375 mL
2	garlic cloves, minced	2
½ cup	packed fresh basil leaves, finely chopped	125 mL
1 tsp	pepper	5 mL
½ tsp	salt	2 mL
2	green onions, finely chopped	2
¼ cup	PRIMO 100% Pure Olive Oil	50 mL
¾ lb	PRIMO Spaghetti	375 g

- In a large bowl, stir together tomatoes, mozzarella cubes, garlic, basil, pepper, salt and green onions. Drizzle with oil and toss to combine. Let stand 30 minutes.

- Meanwhile, in a large pot of boiling, salted water, cook pasta 8-10 minutes, or until tender but firm. Drain and toss immediately with marinated tomato mixture. Serve with freshly ground black pepper.

PREPARATION TIME: 10 MINUTES
MARINATING TIME: 30 MINUTES
COOKING TIME: 10 MINUTES
MAKES 4 SERVINGS

LINGUINE con SALSA al GORGONZOLA

LINGUINE WITH GORGONZOLA CREAM SAUCE

1 cup	table cream (18% MF)	250 mL
1 tbsp	butter	15 mL
6 oz	Gorgonzola cheese, crumbled	175 g
½ tsp	pepper	2 mL
¾ lb	PRIMO Linguine Fine	375 mL
¼ cup	*each* PRIMO 100% Grated Parmesan Cheese and toasted, chopped pecans	50 mL

- Place cream, butter, Gorgonzola and pepper in skillet over medium-low heat. Heat gently until cheese melts and sauce thickens.

- In a large pot of boiling, salted water, cook pasta 7 minutes, or until tender but firm. Drain and toss with Gorgonzola sauce and Parmesan. Garnish with toasted pecans and serve.

PREPARATION TIME: 5 MINUTES
COOKING TIME: 10 MINUTES
MAKES 4 SERVINGS

Linguine
IN WILD MUSHROOM SAUCE

2	pkgs (10 g) dried porcini mushrooms	2
1 cup	hot water	250 mL
2 tbsp	butter	25 mL
½ cup	finely chopped green onion	125 mL
6 cups	sliced fresh mushrooms	1.5 L
1 tbsp	all-purpose flour	15 mL
1 tsp	salt	5 mL
¼ tsp	freshly ground black pepper	1 mL
1 cup	table cream (18% MF)	250 mL
1 lb	PRIMO Linguine	450 g
¼ cup	chopped fresh parsley	50 mL

• Soak dried mushrooms in hot water for 30 minutes. Drain in a sieve lined with a coffee filter, reserving liquid. Slice softened mushrooms into thin strips.

• In large skillet, melt butter over medium-high heat. Add green onions and fresh mushrooms; cook 5 minutes or until mushrooms begin to release liquid.

• Reduce heat to medium-low. Add flour, salt and pepper; cook 1 minute, stirring constantly. Add the reserved mushroom liquid and cook uncovered 5 minutes, or until liquid has thickened slightly.

• Stir in cream and cook 10 minutes, or until sauce coats back of spoon. Stir in parsley and softened mushrooms.

• Meanwhile, in a large pot of boiling, salted water, cook linguine 8-10 minutes, or until tender but firm. Drain and toss sauce with hot pasta. Serve immediately.

PREPARATION TIME: 20 MINUTES
SOAKING TIME: 30 MINUTES
COOKING TIME: 20 MINUTES
MAKES 4 SERVINGS

HEARTY
SIMMERED SAUCES

OSSO BUCO

2 tbsp	PRIMO Vegetable Oil	25 mL
2 lbs	centre-cut veal shanks	900 g
1 tbsp	butter	15 mL
2	carrots, finely chopped	2
2	celery stalks, finely chopped	2
1	onion, finely chopped	1
1	can (28 oz/796 mL) PRIMO Tomatoes, drained	1
1½ cups	chicken stock	375 mL
1	bay leaf	1
½ tsp	*each* salt, pepper, dried basil and thyme	2 mL
⅓ cup	finely chopped fresh parsley	75 mL
2	garlic cloves, minced	2
4 cups	PRIMO Gnocchi	1 L
	zest of 1 lemon, minced	

In large, heavy saucepan, heat oil over medium-high heat. Brown shanks in batches, approximately 1 minute per side. Remove from pan and set aside.

Add butter to pan and reduce heat to medium. Add carrots, celery and onion; cook 15 minutes, or until softened and lightly browned, stirring occasionally.

Stir in tomatoes, chicken stock, bay leaf, salt, pepper, basil, thyme and browned veal shanks; bring to a boil. Reduce heat to low, cover and cook 2 hours, or until meat is very tender.

Combine parsley, garlic and lemon zest; set aside.

Meanwhile, in a large pot of boiling, salted water, cook gnocchi 8-10 minutes, or until tender but firm; drain.

Serve osso buco over gnocchi sprinkled with the parsley mixture.

NOTE: The aromatic parsley-garlic-lemon zest mixture which is sprinkled on top of the osso buco is called gremolata.

PREPARATION TIME: 10 MINUTES
COOKING TIME: 2 HOURS, 20 MINUTES
MAKES 4 SERVINGS

POLLO alla CACCIATORA

CHICKEN CACCIATORE

*A classic Italian dish that is quite possibly made as many ways
as there are cooks who make it.*

1 tbsp	PRIMO Vegetable Oil	15 mL
6	chicken thighs, skin removed	6
pinch	*each* salt and pepper	pinch
1	large onion, chopped	1
2	*each* carrots and celery stalks, sliced	2
1½ cups	sliced fresh mushrooms	375 mL
1 cup	chopped green pepper	250 mL
3	garlic cloves, minced	3
½ tsp	*each* dried basil and oregano	2 mL
¼ tsp	red pepper flakes	1 mL
¼ cup	white wine (optional)	50 mL
1	can (28 oz/796 mL) PRIMO Tomatoes	1
2 tbsp	PRIMO Tomato Paste	25 mL
¼ cup	chopped fresh parsley	50 mL
1 lb	PRIMO Spaghetti	450 g

• In dutch oven, heat oil over medium-high heat. Sprinkle chicken thighs evenly with salt and pepper; brown each side 4 minutes. Remove from pot and set aside.

• Reduce heat to medium; add onion, carrots, celery, mushrooms, green pepper and garlic. Cook 10 minutes or until carrots are almost tender. Stir in basil, oregano and red pepper flakes; cook 1 minute, stirring constantly.

• Stir in wine (if using), tomatoes and tomato paste; return chicken to pot. Bring to a boil over medium heat. Reduce heat to low, cover and cook 20 minutes, stirring occasionally. Remove lid and cook 15 minutes, or until sauce thickens slightly. Stir in parsley.

• Meanwhile, in a large pot of boiling, salted water, cook pasta 8-10 minutes, or until tender but firm. Drain pasta and toss with 1 cup (250 mL) of sauce. Place pasta on serving platter and top with remaining sauce and chicken.

PREPARATION TIME: 20 MINUTES
COOKING TIME: 55 MINUTES
MAKES 6 SERVINGS

SALSA per SPAGHETTI CASERECCIA

HOMEMADE SPAGHETTI SAUCE

1½ lb	lean ground beef	675 g
1	*each* large onion and green pepper, chopped	1
5	garlic cloves, minced	5
1 cup	sliced fresh mushrooms	250 mL
2 tsp	*each* dried basil and oregano	10 mL
½ tsp	*each* dried thyme and rosemary	2 mL
2	bay leaves	2
1	can (28 oz/ 796 mL) PRIMO Tomatoes	1
1	can (14 oz/398 mL) PRIMO Tomato Sauce	1
2	cans (5 ½ oz/156 mL) PRIMO Tomato Paste	2
¼ cup	red wine	50 mL
2 tbsp	PRIMO 100% Grated Parmesan Cheese	25 mL
2 tsp	granulated sugar	10 mL
1 lb	PRIMO Spaghetti	450 g

• In large saucepan, brown beef over medium-high heat, breaking up any large pieces.

• Reduce heat to medium. Stir in onion, green pepper, garlic and mushrooms; cook 10 minutes until vegetables are softened. Stir in all herbs; cook 1 minute.

• Add tomatoes, tomato sauce and paste, wine, Parmesan and sugar. Bring to a boil over medium heat. Reduce heat and simmer 45 minutes or until meat is tender.

• Meanwhile, in a large pot of boiling, salted water, cook spaghetti 8-10 minutes, or until tender but firm. Drain pasta.

• Remove bay leaves and pour sauce over hot pasta. Sprinkle with extra Parmesan cheese and serve.

PREPARATION TIME: 20 MINUTES
COOKING TIME: 1 HOUR
MAKES 6 SERVINGS

BEEF AND PEPPER RAGOUT

2 tbsp	all-purpose flour	25 mL
¾ tsp	*each* salt and pepper	4 mL
1½ lb	stewing beef, trimmed	675 g
2 tbsp	PRIMO Vegetable Oil	25 mL
2	large onions, cut into wedges	2
4	garlic cloves, sliced	4
1	large carrot, sliced	1
½ tsp	*each* dried basil and oregano	2 mL
1	bay leaf	1
1	can (28 oz/796 mL) PRIMO Tomatoes	1
½ cup	red wine	125 mL
¼ cup	PRIMO Tomato Paste	50 mL
1	*each* red and green pepper, cut into cubes	1
¼ cup	chopped fresh parsley	50 mL

———•———

● In bowl, combine flour, ¼ tsp (1 mL) salt and ¼ tsp (1 mL) pepper. Toss beef with flour mixture.

● In large saucepan, heat 1 tbsp (15 mL) oil over medium-high heat. Brown beef in batches, about 5 minutes each, using as much oil as needed. Remove from pan and set aside.

● Cook onion, garlic and carrot 5 minutes. Stir in remaining salt, pepper and herbs; cook 1 minute, stirring constantly. Add tomatoes, wine and tomato paste; stir to combine. Return beef to pan. Bring to a boil; reduce heat to low, cover and cook 1 hour. Stir occasionally.

● Stir in peppers; cook uncovered 45 minutes to 1 hour, or until tender. Remove and discard bay leaf.

● Remove from heat and stir in parsley. Serve over egg noodles, polenta or steamed rice.

PREPARATION TIME: 20 MINUTES
COOKING TIME: 2 HOURS
MAKES 6 SERVINGS

NEW SPAGHETTI AND MEATBALLS

Spaghetti and meatballs get a new twist with ground chicken.

MEATBALLS:

1 lb	ground chicken	450 g
1	small onion, finely chopped	1
½ tsp	salt	2 mL
¼ tsp	pepper	1 mL
2 tbsp	PRIMO Vegetable Oil	25 mL

TOMATO SAUCE:

1	onion, chopped	1
2	garlic cloves, minced	2
1	can (28 oz/796 mL) PRIMO Tomatoes, crushed	1
1	can (14 oz/398 mL) PRIMO Tomato Sauce	1
2 tbsp	PRIMO Tomato Paste	25 mL
1 tsp	dried oregano	5 mL
½ tsp	dried basil	2 mL
¼ cup	chopped fresh parsley	50 mL
1 lb	PRIMO Spaghetti	450 g
½ cup	shredded Cheddar cheese	125 mL

• Stir together chicken, onion, salt and pepper. Divide chicken mixture into balls.

• In a large saucepan, heat oil over medium-high heat. Cook meatballs in batches, 5-7 minutes each, or until browned on all sides. Remove, drain off fat, and set aside.

• In same saucepan, cook onion and garlic over medium heat 3-5 minutes, or until tender. Stir in tomatoes, tomato sauce and paste, oregano and basil; bring to a boil over medium heat. Reduce heat and simmer 35 minutes, or until sauce thickens.

• Stir in parsley and meatballs; cook 10 minutes or until meatballs are cooked through.

• In a large pot of boiling, salted water, cook pasta 8-10 minutes, or until tender but firm. Drain pasta.

• Spoon sauce and meatballs over pasta. Sprinkle with Cheddar cheese and serve immediately.

PREPARATION TIME: 20 MINUTES
COOKING TIME: 1 HOUR
MAKES 6 SERVINGS

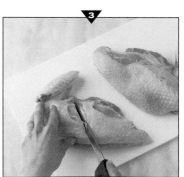

Removing the legs – Push the leg outwards to loosen joint; with a sharp knife, sever leg at joint and remove.

Removing the back – With sharp kitchen shears or knife, cut through ribs along each side of backbone and remove.

Splitting the breast – Flatten whole breast against work surface to break breast bone. Cut breast bone in half. Remove wing tips. Cut each breast in half diagonally.

COQ AU VIN

This classic French dish is simple and comforting.

1 cup	pearl onions	250 mL
1 tbsp	PRIMO Vegetable Oil	15 mL
3 tbsp	butter	45 mL
3	bacon strips, finely chopped	3
2½ cups	quartered mushrooms	625 mL
1	4 lb (1.8 kg) chicken, cut into 8 pieces	1
	salt and pepper	
¼ cup	all-purpose flour	50 mL
3 cups	dry white wine	750 mL
1 lb	PRIMO Fettuccine	450 g
¼ cup	chopped fresh parsley	50 mL

• Blanch onions in boiling water; refresh in cold water and peel off skins. Trim ends and set aside.

• In large saucepan, heat oil and 1 tbsp (15 mL) butter over medium-high heat. Add bacon and cook 2 minutes, or until browned, stirring constantly.

• Add pearl onions and mushrooms; cook 5 minutes or until browned. Remove bacon and vegetables from pan.

• Season chicken with salt and pepper. Brown chicken in batches, approximately 1-2 minutes per side. Remove from pan and set aside.

• Reduce heat to medium-low; melt remaining butter in pan. Stir in flour and whisk 1 minute. Gradually add wine, whisking constantly. Increase heat to medium; stir until mixture comes to a boil.

• Return chicken leg pieces, bacon, onions and mushrooms to pan. Reduce heat to low, cover and cook 30 minutes. Add chicken breast pieces, replace lid and cook another 30 minutes.

• Meanwhile, in a pot of boiling, salted water, cook pasta 8 to 10 minutes, or until tender but firm. Drain pasta.

• Pour the coq au vin over pasta, sprinkle with parsley and serve.

TIP: You can substitute the 4 lb chicken with two 2 lb (900 g) packages of pre-cut chicken pieces.

PREPARATION TIME: 15 MINUTES
COOKING TIME: 1 HOUR, 20 MINUTES
MAKES 4 – 6 SERVINGS

STIFADO

GREEK BEEF STEW

⅓ cup	**PRIMO Vegetable Oil**	75 mL
2 lbs	**stewing beef or lamb, trimmed and cut into cubes**	900 g
2	**onions, chopped**	2
3	**garlic cloves, minced**	3
1	**can (28 oz/796 mL) PRIMO Tomatoes, crushed**	1
1 tsp	*each* **ground cinnamon and dried oregano**	5 mL
¼ tsp	**crushed red pepper flakes**	1 mL
3	**carrots, sliced**	3
3	**potatoes, peeled and cut into cubes**	3
3 tbsp	**lemon juice**	45 mL
1	**can (19 oz/540 mL) PRIMO Red Kidney Beans, rinsed and drained**	1
1	**pkg (375 g) PRIMO Medium Egg Noodles**	1
	salt and pepper to taste	

—•—

● In large saucepan, heat ¼ cup (50 mL) of oil over medium-high heat. Cook beef in batches for 2 minutes, or until well browned on all sides; set aside.

● Reduce heat to medium and add remaining oil. Add onion and garlic; cook 3 minutes or until softened.

● Return beef to pan; add tomatoes, cinnamon, oregano and red pepper flakes. Bring to a boil, reduce heat to low, cover and cook 1 hour.

● Stir in carrots and cover. Cook 25 minutes, stirring occasionally. Add potatoes, cover, and cook another 25 minutes. Stir in lemon juice and kidney beans.

● Meanwhile, in a large pot of boiling, salted water, cook egg noodles 10 minutes or until tender. Drain, top with stifado and serve.

PREPARATION TIME: 15 MINUTES
COOKING TIME: 2 HOURS, 10 MINUTES
MAKES 6 SERVINGS

BOLOGNESE SAUCE

1 tbsp	**PRIMO 100% Pure Olive Oil**	15 mL
2	**carrots, chopped**	2
2	**celery stalks, chopped**	2
1	**onion, chopped**	1
1 lb	**lean ground beef**	450 g
½ tsp	*each* **salt and pepper**	2 mL
1 cup	**dry wine, red or white**	250 mL
1	**can (28 oz/796 mL) PRIMO Tomatoes**	1
1	*each* **bay leaf and whole dried red chili pepper**	1
pinch	**ground nutmeg**	pinch
2 tbsp	**table cream (18% MF)**	25 mL
1 lb	**PRIMO Rigatoni**	450 g
	PRIMO 100% Grated Parmesan Cheese	

• In a large saucepan, heat oil over medium heat. Add carrots, celery and onion; cook 10 minutes or until vegetables soften and begin to brown. Stir occasionally.

• Add beef, salt and pepper; cook 5 minutes or until meat is cooked through, stirring constantly. Add wine and cook 10 minutes, or until most of liquid has evaporated. Stir occasionally.

• Stir in tomatoes, bay leaf, chili pepper, nutmeg and cream; bring to a boil. Reduce heat to low and cook 2 hours, stirring occasionally.

• Meanwhile, in a large pot of boiling, salted water, cook pasta 12-14 minutes, or until tender but firm. Drain and top with sauce. Sprinkle with Parmesan and serve.

PREPARATION TIME: 10 MINUTES
COOKING TIME: 2 HOURS, 30 MINUTES
MAKES 6 SERVINGS

BEAUTIFULLY
BAKED CASSEROLES

SEAFOOD LASAGNE

12	PRIMO Lasagne Noodles	12
1	container (475 g) light ricotta	1
½ cup	PRIMO 100% Grated Parmesan Cheese	125 mL
⅓ cup	table cream (18% MF)	75 mL
½ cup	butter	125 mL
2 cups	chopped fennel	500 mL
1	onion, chopped	1
½ cup	all-purpose flour	125 mL
4 cups	milk	1 L
1 lb	cooked seafood (shrimp, scallops, lobster, clams or mussels)	450 g
1 cup	shredded mozzarella cheese	250 mL

• In a large pot of salted, boiling water, cook lasagne noodles 10-12 minutes or until tender. Rinse under cold water, drain and set aside.

• In bowl, stir together ricotta, Parmesan and cream; set aside.

• In large, heavy-bottomed saucepan melt butter over medium heat. Add fennel and onion; reduce heat to medium-low, and cook 10 minutes, or until softened. Add flour and cook 1 minute, stirring constantly. Gradually add milk, whisking constantly.

• Bring mixture to a boil over medium heat, stirring constantly. Reduce heat to low and simmer 10 minutes or until thickened, stirring occasionally. Remove 1 cup (250 mL) of sauce and set aside. Add seafood to simmering sauce and cook 30 seconds, or until seafood is slightly warmed, stirring constantly.

• Spread ¼ cup (50 mL) of reserved white sauce in bottom of a 13 × 9-in (3 L) baking dish. Layer with 3 lasagne noodles. Spoon ½ of the seafood sauce on top of noodles. Layer with 3 more lasagne noodles.

• Spoon all of ricotta mixture evenly over lasagne. Top with 3 more lasagne noodles. Spoon remaining seafood sauce on top and cover with last 3 lasagne noodles. Pour remaining ¾ cup (175 mL) of reserved white sauce on top; sprinkle with mozzarella.

• Bake at 350°F (180°C) for 25 minutes, or until heated through and mozzarella is melted.

PREPARATION TIME: 20 MINUTES
COOKING TIME: 35 MINUTES
BAKING TIME: 25 MINUTES
MAKES 12 SERVINGS

CHICKEN TETTRAZINI

2 tbsp	butter	25 mL
1	onion, chopped	1
3	garlic cloves, minced	3
2	celery stalks, sliced	2
3 cups	mushrooms, sliced	750 mL
½ tsp	*each* salt, pepper and dried thyme	2 mL
pinch	cayenne	pinch
¼ cup	all-purpose flour	50 mL
2 cups	milk	500 mL
1½ cups	chicken stock	375 mL
½ cup	white wine	125 mL
1	pkg (375 g) PRIMO Broad Egg Noodles	1
4 cups	chopped, cooked chicken or turkey	1 L
⅓ cup	*each* PRIMO 100% Grated Parmesan Cheese and chopped fresh parsley	75 mL
1 cup	fresh breadcrumbs	250 mL
2 tbsp	chopped almonds	25 mL

• In a large, heavy-bottomed saucepan, melt 1 tbsp (15 mL) of butter over medium heat. Add onion, 2 garlic cloves and celery; cook 5-7 minutes or until softened. Stir in mushrooms, salt, pepper, thyme and cayenne; cook 10-12 minutes or until mushrooms release liquid.

• Stir in flour; cook 1 minute, stirring constantly. Whisk in milk, stock and wine; whisk until lumps disappear. Cook 12-15 minutes, or until mushroom sauce comes to a boil and thickens, whisking frequently.

• Meanwhile, in a large pot of boiling, salted water, cook egg noodles 8-9 minutes or until tender. Drain and stir into mushroom sauce; add chicken, ¼ cup (50 mL) of Parmesan and ¼ cup (50 mL) of parsley. Pour into a 13 × 9-in (3 L) baking dish.

• In a small skillet, melt remaining butter over low heat. Stir in remaining garlic and cook 2 minutes. Add breadcrumbs, almonds, remaining parsley and Parmesan; toss well to coat.

• Sprinkle breadcrumb mixture evenly over tettrazini in baking dish. Bake at 350°F (180°C) for 30 minutes, or until sauce is bubbling and breadcrumb mixture is golden brown.

TIP: You can prepare this casserole ahead of time. It keeps in the refrigerator for 1 day, and in the freezer for 2 weeks. If frozen, thaw for 24-48 hours in the refrigerator.

PREPARATION TIME: 1 HOUR
COOKING TIME: 40 MINUTES
BAKING TIME: 30 MINUTES
MAKES 8-10 SERVINGS

POLENTA PASTICCIATA

POLENTA WITH SAUSAGES AND CHEESE

POLENTA:

7 cups	water	1.75 L
1 tsp	salt	5 mL
1	small onion, finely chopped	1
1½ cups	PRIMO Cornmeal	375 mL
¼ cup	PRIMO 100% Grated Parmesan Cheese	50 mL

SAUSAGES:

1 tbsp	PRIMO 100% Pure Olive Oil	15 mL
1	onion, finely chopped	1
1	can (28 oz/796 mL) PRIMO Tomatoes, puréed	1
¼ cup	chopped fresh basil (or 2 tsp (10 mL) dried)	50 mL
1 lb	Italian sausages, cut into ¼-in (5-mm) slices	450 g
½ tsp	pepper	2 mL
½ cup	PRIMO 100% Grated Parmesan Cheese	125 mL

• In large saucepan, bring water, salt and onion to a boil over medium-high heat. Slowly add cornmeal in a thin steady stream, whisking constantly.

• Reduce heat to medium-low; stir constantly 20-25 minutes or until polenta thickens. Stir in Parmesan. Pour half of polenta into a greased 11 × 7-in (2 L) baking dish; pour remaining polenta onto a greased 13 × 9-in rimmed baking sheet. Cool.

• In a shallow saucepan, heat oil over medium heat. Cook onion 3-5 minutes or until softened. Stir in tomatoes, basil, sausages and pepper; bring to a boil over medium heat. Reduce heat to medium-low and simmer 30 minutes, or until sauce thickens. Remove from heat.

• Spoon half of sausage sauce over polenta in baking dish. Sprinkle with ¼ cup (50 mL) of Parmesan. Cut polenta on baking sheet and fit over sausage sauce. Spoon remaining sauce over polenta. Cut remaining polenta into triangles and arrange on top. Sprinkle with remaining Parmesan.

• Bake at 350°F (180°C) for 30-35 minutes or until hot and bubbly. Let stand 10 minutes before serving.

PREPARATION TIME: 20 MINUTES
COOKING TIME: 1 HOUR
BAKING TIME: 30-35 MINUTES
MAKES 6 SERVINGS

TEX-MEX PASTA CASSEROLE

A colourful and flavourful casserole that is wonderful for a crowd.

½ lb	spicy Italian Sausage, sliced	225 g
1	large onion, chopped	1
½	green pepper, chopped	½
2	garlic cloves, minced	2
2 tsp	chili powder	10 mL
½ tsp	*each* ground cumin and dried oregano	2 mL
pinch	hot pepper flakes	pinch
2	cans (14 oz/398 mL) PRIMO Tomato Sauce	2
4 cups	PRIMO Rotini	1 L
1 cup	*each* shredded old Cheddar cheese and corn kernels	250 mL
¾ cup	PRIMO Pitted Black Olives, sliced	175 mL
1	can (19 oz/540 mL) PRIMO Kidney Beans, rinsed and drained	1
¼ cup	chopped fresh parsley	50 mL

———•———

● In a non-stick skillet, brown sausage slices over medium-high heat. Remove and set aside.

● Reduce heat to medium; cook onion, green pepper and garlic 5 minutes, or until softened. Stir in chili powder, cumin, oregano and hot pepper flakes; cook 1 minute. Pour in tomato sauce and stir to combine. Bring to a boil, reduce heat to low and simmer 15 minutes.

● Meanwhile, in a large pot of boiling, salted water, cook pasta 8-10 minutes, or until still firm to the bite. Drain pasta.

● In a large bowl, combine tomato sauce, pasta, ¾ cup (175 mL) of Cheddar cheese, corn, olives, kidney beans, cooked sausage and parsley. Spoon into a casserole dish and sprinkle with remaining Cheddar.

● Cover and bake at 350°F (180°C) for 25 minutes. Uncover and bake 10 more minutes, or until heated through.

TIP: Substitute corn kernels with 12 baby corn cobs, if desired.

PREPARATION TIME: 20 MINUTES
COOKING TIME: 20 MINUTES
BAKING TIME: 35 MINUTES
MAKES 6-8 SERVINGS

LASAGNE ROLL-UPS

Lasagne roll-ups are perfect for a buffet.

½ lb	Italian sausages, casings removed and crumbled	225 g
1	onion, chopped	1
2	garlic cloves, minced	2
1	can (28 oz/796 mL) PRIMO Tomatoes, crushed	1
2 tbsp	PRIMO Tomato Paste	25 mL
1 tsp	dried oregano	5 mL
½ tsp	dried basil	2 mL
10	PRIMO Lasagne Noodles	10
1	pkg (300 g) frozen chopped spinach, thawed and well-drained	1
2 cups	ricotta cheese	500 mL
½ cup	PRIMO 100% Grated Parmesan Cheese	125 mL
1½ cups	shredded mozzarella cheese	375 mL
1	egg	1
½ tsp	salt	2 mL
¼ tsp	pepper	1 mL

• In skillet, brown sausage 5-7 minutes over high heat. Break up any large pieces and drain fat if necessary. Reduce heat to medium, add onion and garlic to sausages, and cook 3 minutes, or until softened.

• Stir in tomatoes, tomato paste, oregano and basil; bring to a boil over medium heat. Reduce heat and simmer 15 minutes, or until sauce thickens slightly. Remove from heat and set aside.

• Meanwhile, in a large pot of boiling, salted water, cook lasagne 14-16 minutes, or until tender but firm. Refresh in cold water, drain and set aside.

• In bowl, stir together spinach, ricotta, Parmesan, 1 cup (250 mL) of mozzarella, egg, salt and pepper until thoroughly combined.

• Spread ½ cup (125 mL) of tomato-sausage sauce on bottom of an 11 × 7-in (2 L) baking dish.

• Divide and spread ricotta mixture onto each lasagne noodle. Spoon 1 tbsp (15 mL) of tomato-sausage sauce down middle of each coated noodle. Roll up lasagne noodles jelly-roll style, and place seam side down in baking dish.

• Spoon remaining sauce evenly over rolls and sprinkle with remaining mozzarella. Bake at 350°F (180°C) for 30-35 minutes or until hot and bubbly. Each roll is 1 serving.

PREPARATION TIME: 30 MINUTES
COOKING TIME: 25 MINUTES
BAKING TIME: 30-35 MINUTES
MAKES 8-10 SERVINGS

In large bowl, combine pasta, pesto and cooked onion.

Remove giblets, neck and excess fat from chicken. Stuff chicken with pasta mixture.

Truss chicken with string; rub with remaining olive oil, salt and pepper.

PASTA-STUFFED ROAST CHICKEN

There's nothing like the tantalizing smell of roast chicken!

2 cups	packed fresh basil leaves	500 mL
4	garlic cloves, minced	4
¼ cup	pine nuts, toasted	50 mL
1 tsp	salt	5 mL
¼ tsp	pepper	1 mL
½ cup	*each* PRIMO 100% Pure Olive Oil and PRIMO 100% Grated Parmesan Cheese	125 mL
1½ cups	PRIMO Macaroni	375 mL
2 tbsp	PRIMO 100% Pure Olive Oil	25 mL
1	onion, chopped	1
1	5 lb (2.2 kg) roasting chicken	1
	salt and pepper	

—————•—————

• Place basil, garlic, pine nuts, salt and pepper in food processor; mix until finely chopped. Add olive oil gradually; combine until mixture is smooth. Add Parmesan; pulse on and off until thoroughly combined.

• In a pot of boiling, salted water, cook pasta 8-10 minutes, or until tender but firm. Drain and toss with pesto.

• In skillet, heat 1 tbsp (15 mL) of olive oil over medium heat. Add onion and cook 3 minutes, or until softened. Stir into pasta.

• Preheat oven to 450°F (230°C). Remove giblets, neck and excess fat from chicken cavity; discard. Stuff chicken with pasta mixture and truss chicken. Rub chicken with remaining olive oil, salt and pepper.

• Place on rack in roasting pan. Roast uncovered 30 minutes; reduce heat to 400°F (200°C), and roast 1 hour.

• Test by skewering leg at thickest point; juices should run clear and thermometer registers 185°F (85°C). Remove from oven and let chicken stand 10 minutes before carving.

PREPARATION TIME: 20 MINUTES
COOKING TIME: 15 MINUTES
ROASTING TIME: 1 HOUR, 30 MINUTES
MAKES 4 SERVINGS

SWISS MANICOTTI

8	PRIMO Manicotti Noodles	8
¼ cup	butter	50 mL
2 cups	finely chopped fresh mushrooms	500 mL
4	green onions, finely chopped	4
1	garlic clove, minced	1
2 cups	finely chopped cooked chicken or turkey	500 mL
2 cups	shredded Swiss cheese	500 mL
¼ cup	PRIMO 100% Grated Parmesan Cheese	50 mL
¾ tsp	pepper	4 mL
1	egg	1
2 tbsp	all-purpose flour	25 mL
2 cups	milk	500 mL
¼ cup	white wine (optional)	50 mL
1 tsp	Dijon mustard	5 mL
½ tsp	salt	2 mL

• In a large pot of boiling, salted water, cook manicotti 16-18 minutes or until tender. Refresh in cold water, drain and set aside.

• Meanwhile, in a heavy saucepan, melt 2 tbsp (25 mL) of butter over medium heat. Add mushrooms, green onions and garlic; cook 3 minutes or until mushrooms begin to release liquid. Remove from heat.

• In a large bowl, stir together mushroom mixture, chicken, ½ cup (125 mL) Swiss cheese, Parmesan and ¼ tsp (1 mL) pepper. When cool, mix in egg and set aside.

• In same saucepan, melt remaining butter over medium heat. Stir in flour and cook 1 minute, stirring constantly.

• Gradually whisk in milk; bring to a boil over medium heat, whisking constantly. Remove from heat and whisk in 1 cup (250 mL) of Swiss cheese, wine (if using), Dijon mustard, salt and remaining pepper.

• Spread ½ cup (125 mL) of cheese sauce on bottom of a 13 × 9-in (3 L) baking dish. Divide and stuff filling into manicotti; place in baking dish.

• Spoon remaining cheese sauce over manicotti and sprinkle with remaining Swiss cheese. Bake at 350°F (180°C) for 30 minutes, or until heated through.

PREPARATION TIME: 30 MINUTES
COOKING TIME: 20 MINUTES
BAKING TIME: 30 MINUTES
MAKES 4 SERVINGS

LASAGNE CON CARNE

LASAGNE WITH MEAT

12	PRIMO Lasagne Noodles	12
1	recipe Bolognese Sauce (p. 144)	1
¼ cup	*each* butter and all-purpose flour	50 mL
3 cups	2% milk	750 mL
pinch	*each* salt, pepper and nutmeg	pinch
⅓ cup	PRIMO 100% Grated Parmesan Cheese	75 mL

● In a large pot of boiling, salted water, cook lasagne 18-20 minutes or until tender. Place noodles in bowl of cold water and drain; set aside.

● In a heavy-bottomed pot, melt butter over medium-low heat. Add flour and cook 1 minute, stirring constantly. Whisk in milk gradually. Increase heat to medium and cook 5 minutes, or until mixture comes to a boil, whisking constantly.

● Reduce heat to low; stir in salt, pepper and nutmeg. Cook 10 minutes or until mixture thickens, stirring occasionally. Remove from heat.

● Spread ½ cup (125 mL) white sauce in bottom of a 13 × 9-in (3 L) baking dish; layer with 3 noodles. Layer ½ of meat sauce on top and cover with 3 more noodles. Repeat layers, top with remaining white sauce and sprinkle with Parmesan.

● Bake at 350°F (180°C) for 25 minutes, or until heated through and Parmesan browns.

PREPARATION TIME: 10 MINUTES
COOKING TIME: 30 MINUTES
BAKING TIME: 25 MINUTES
MAKES 12 SERVINGS

TUNA CASSEROLE

1 tbsp	**PRIMO Vegetable Oil**	15 mL
1 cup	**sliced fresh mushrooms**	250 mL
½ cup	*each* **chopped onion, green pepper and celery**	125 mL
1 cup	**milk**	250 mL
1	**can (10 oz/284 mL) cream of mushroom soup**	1
1 tsp	**Dijon mustard**	5 mL
3 cups	**PRIMO Small Shells**	750 mL
½ cup	**frozen peas**	125 mL
2	**cans (7 oz/199 mL) PRIMO Solid Light Tuna, drained and flaked**	2
¼ cup	*each* **PRIMO Italian Style Bread Crumbs and PRIMO 100% Grated Parmesan Cheese**	50 mL

• Heat oil in skillet over medium heat. Add mushrooms, onion, green pepper and celery; cook 5 minutes or until softened.

• In bowl, whisk together milk, mushroom soup and mustard; stir in mushroom mixture and set aside.

• In a large pot of boiling, salted water, cook pasta 9 minutes, or until tender but firm. Drain and stir into milk mixture; add peas and tuna. Spoon into a 2-quart (2 L) casserole dish.

• Combine bread crumbs and Parmesan; sprinkle over casserole. Bake at 350°F (190°C) for 30 minutes, or until hot and bubbling.

PREPARATION TIME: 10 MINUTES
COOKING TIME: 15 MINUTES
BAKING TIME: 30 MINUTES
MAKES 4 SERVINGS

CHICKEN PARMESAN

TOMATO SAUCE:

1 tbsp	**PRIMO 100% Pure Olive Oil**	15 mL
1	**small onion, chopped**	1
3	**garlic cloves, minced**	3
¼ tsp	**pepper**	1 mL
1	**can (28 oz/796 mL) PRIMO Crushed Tomatoes**	1

BREADED CHICKEN:

4	**boneless chicken breasts**	4
½ cup	**PRIMO Breadcrumbs**	125 mL
¼ cup	*each* **PRIMO 100% Grated Parmesan Cheese and all-purpose flour**	50 mL
2	**eggs, beaten**	2
1 cup	**shredded mozzarella cheese**	250 mL
¾ lb	**PRIMO Spaghetti**	375 g
¼ cup	**chopped fresh parsley**	50 mL

—•—

• Heat oil in saucepan over medium heat. Add onion, garlic and pepper; cook 3-5 minutes or until softened. Add tomatoes and stir to combine. Heat until tomato sauce comes to a boil. Remove from heat and set aside.

• Trim all visible fat from chicken. Place breasts between two pieces of waxed paper and pound until ½-in (1-cm) thick.

• In shallow dish, combine breadcrumbs and Parmesan. Dip each breast into flour, then egg and finally in breadcrumb mixture. Place on baking sheet. Bake at 400°F (200°C) for 10 minutes.

• Spoon ¼ cup (50 mL) of tomato sauce over each breast; sprinkle each breast with ¼ cup (50 mL) of mozzarella cheese. Bake 10 minutes or until cheese melts.

• Meanwhile, in a large pot of boiling, salted water, cook pasta 8-10 minutes, or until tender but firm. Drain pasta.

• Toss pasta with remaining sauce and parsley. Serve with chicken.

TIP: If you want to make this dish ahead of time, bread chicken breasts and place them on a baking rack over a baking sheet. They keep up to 4 hours in the refrigerator.

PREPARATION TIME: 25 MINUTES
COOKING TIME: 10 MINUTES
BAKING TIME: 20 MINUTES
MAKES 4 SERVINGS

Place chicken breasts between waxed paper and pound until $^1/_2$-in (1-cm) thick.

Dip each breast into flour, then egg, and finally in breadcrumb mixture. Bake for 10 minutes.

Spoon tomato sauce over each breast and sprinkle with mozzarella cheese. Bake until cheese melts.

PASTITSIO

2¾ cups	**PRIMO Macaroni**	675 mL

MEAT SAUCE:

1 tbsp	**PRIMO 100% Pure Olive Oil**	15 mL
1	**onion, chopped**	1
2	**garlic cloves, minced**	2
1½ lb	**lean ground beef or lamb**	675 g
1	**can (28 oz/796 mL) PRIMO Tomatoes**	1
2 tbsp	**PRIMO Tomato Paste**	25 mL
1½ tsp	**dried oregano**	7 mL
1 tsp	**ground cinnamon**	5 mL
pinch	**cayenne pepper**	pinch
¼ tsp	*each* **salt and pepper**	1 mL

CUSTARD:

⅓ cup	*each* **butter and all-purpose flour**	75 mL
5 cups	**2% milk**	1.25 L
½ tsp	**ground nutmeg**	2 mL
1	**bay leaf**	1
3	**eggs**	3
½ cup	*each* **PRIMO 100% Grated Parmesan Cheese and PRIMO 100% Grated Romano Cheese**	125 mL

• In large pot of boiling, salted water, cook pasta 8-10 minutes, or until tender but firm. Drain, rinse lightly, drain and set aside.

• Heat oil in large saucepan over medium heat. Cook onion and garlic 3 minutes until softened. Add beef and cook 5 minutes, or until browned.

• Stir in tomatoes, tomato paste, oregano, cinnamon, cayenne, a pinch of salt and pepper; bring to a boil. Reduce heat to medium-low and cook 20 minutes, or until thickened.

• Meanwhile, in large saucepan, melt butter over medium heat. Add flour and cook 1 minute, stirring constantly.

• Add milk, remaining salt and pepper, nutmeg and bay leaf, whisking constantly. Cook 7 minutes, or until mixture comes to a boil, stirring constantly. Reduce heat to low and cook 10 minutes, stirring occasionally. Remove from heat; discard bay leaf.

• Whisk eggs in a bowl. Gradually add 2 cups (500 mL) of hot white sauce to eggs, whisking constantly. Pour mixture into pot of white sauce and whisk thoroughly.

• In a small bowl, combine Parmesan and Romano cheeses.

• Spread half of pasta in bottom of a 13 × 9-in (3 L) baking dish; layer half of white sauce and half of cheese mixture over pasta. Spread all of meat sauce on top. Repeat pasta, white sauce and cheese layers.

• Bake at 400°F (200°C) for 30 minutes, or until browned and bubbly. Let stand 15 minutes before serving.

PREPARATION TIME: 10 MINUTES
COOKING TIME: 50 MINUTES
BAKING TIME: 30 MINUTES
MAKES 12 SERVINGS

SAVOURY NOODLE KUGEL

Served with a green salad and some fresh fruit for dessert,
this is a perfect recipe for lunch or brunch.

½ lb	**PRIMO Medium Egg Noodles**	225 g
2 tbsp	**PRIMO Vegetable Oil**	25 mL
1	**onion, chopped**	1
2 cups	**quartered fresh mushrooms**	500 mL
3	**green onions, chopped**	3
¾ tsp	**salt**	4 mL
¼ tsp	**pepper**	1 mL
1 cup	**low-fat sour cream**	250 mL
2	**eggs, beaten**	2
2 tbsp	**chopped fresh parsley**	25 mL

●In a large pot of boiling, salted water, cook noodles 6-8 minutes, or until tender but firm. Drain, rinse with cold water, drain again and set aside.

●Meanwhile, in a large skillet, heat 1 tbsp (15 mL) of oil over medium heat. Cook onion 3-5 minutes or until softened.

●Heat remaining oil. Add mushrooms, green onions, salt and pepper; cook 8 minutes or until onions begin to brown.

●Remove from heat and stir into cooked noodles; add sour cream, eggs and parsley. Spoon into a greased, 8-in square (1.5 L) baking dish. Bake at 350°F (180°C) for 40-45 minutes or until set. Let stand 10 minutes. Using a serrated knife, cut into squares and serve.

PREPARATION TIME: 10 MINUTES
COOKING TIME: 15 MINUTES
BAKING TIME: 45 MINUTES
MAKES 6 SERVINGS

OLD-FASHIONED MACARONI AND CHEESE

2 cups	PRIMO Macaroni	500 mL
2 tbsp	*each* butter, finely chopped onion and all-purpose flour	25 mL
2 cups	2% milk	500 mL
¼ tsp	*each* salt and pepper	1 mL
3 cups	shredded old Cheddar cheese	750 mL
2 tbsp	*each* PRIMO Italian Style Seasoned Bread Crumbs and PRIMO 100% Grated Parmesan Cheese	25 mL

●In a large pot of boiling, salted water, cook pasta 8-10 minutes, or until tender but firm. Drain and rinse lightly.

●Meanwhile, melt butter in saucepan over medium heat. Add onion and cook 3 minutes, or until softened.

●Add flour and cook 1 minute, stirring constantly. Gradually add milk; stir in salt and pepper. Cook 5 minutes, or until mixture comes to a boil, stirring constantly.

●Reduce heat to low and cook 10 minutes, stirring occasionally. Remove from heat and gradually stir in cheese. Stir in pasta and spoon into a buttered 2-quart (2 L) casserole.

●Combine bread crumbs and Parmesan; sprinkle evenly over top. Bake at 375°F (190°C) for 30 minutes or until bubbly.

PREPARATION TIME: 10 MINUTES
COOKING TIME: 20 MINUTES
BAKING TIME: 30 MINUTES
MAKES 4 SERVINGS

ZUCCHINI AND EGGPLANT LASAGNE

9	**PRIMO Lasagne Noodles**	9

TOMATO SAUCE:

1	**can (28 oz/796 mL) PRIMO Crushed Tomatoes**	1
2	**garlic cloves, minced**	2

CHEESE SAUCE:

2 tbsp	*each* **butter and all-purpose flour**	25 mL
2 cups	**milk**	500 mL
2	**bay leaves**	2
pinch	*each* **nutmeg, salt and pepper**	pinch
1 cup	**shredded Gruyère or Emmenthal cheese**	250 mL

VEGETABLES:

¼ cup	**PRIMO 100% Pure Olive Oil**	50 mL
1 lb	*each* **zucchini and eggplant, thinly sliced**	450 g
½ lb	**mushrooms, sliced**	225 g
¼ tsp	**dried thyme**	1 mL
pinch	*each* **salt and pepper**	pinch

TOPPING:

1½ cups	**shredded mozzarella cheese**	375 mL

● In a glass bowl, stir together tomatoes and garlic; set aside.

● In a heavy-bottomed saucepan, melt butter over medium heat. Stir in flour and cook 1 minute, stirring constantly.

● Gradually whisk in milk, bay leaves, nutmeg, salt and pepper. Bring to a boil over medium heat stirring constantly. Reduce heat; cook 5 minutes. Remove from heat; discard bay leaves; stir in cheese until melted. Set aside.

● In a skillet, heat 1 tbsp (15 mL) of oil over medium-high heat. Cook zucchini and eggplant in separate batches, 7-10 minutes each or until softened. Remove from pan and set aside.

● Heat remaining oil in skillet; add mushrooms, thyme, salt and pepper; cook until liquid has evaporated. Set aside.

● Meanwhile, in a large pot of boiling, salted water, cook lasagne 12-14 minutes, or until tender but firm. Refresh in cold water, drain and set aside.

● Spoon 1 cup (250 mL) of tomato sauce evenly in a 9 × 13-in (2 L) baking dish.

● Layer 3 lasagne noodles over sauce. Spread zucchini evenly over noodles and sprinkle with mushrooms. Spoon cheese sauce evenly over zucchini-mushroom layer and top with 3 more lasagne noodles. Spread eggplant evenly over noodles and top with 1 cup (250 mL) of tomato sauce. Top with last 3 noodles and spread remaining tomato sauce on top; sprinkle with mozzarella cheese.

● Bake at 350°F (180°C) for 30-35 minutes, or until cheese has melted and sauce is bubbly. Let stand 15 minutes before serving.

PREPARATION TIME: 30 MINUTES
COOKING TIME: 30 MINUTES
BAKING TIME: 35 MINUTES
MAKES 8-10 SERVINGS

Stir tomatoes, spaghetti sauce, Worcestershire and hot pepper flakes into cooked vegetables. Cook 1 hour, stirring occasionally.

In large bowl, combine cheeses, eggs, walnuts, parsley, basil, salt and pepper.

Stuff shells with filling and place in prepared dish. Pour remaining sauce over shells and sprinkle with Parmesan.

CHEESE-STUFFED SHELLS

Pressed cottage cheese gives these stuffed shells a meaty texture.

TOMATO SAUCE:

1 tbsp	PRIMO 100% Pure Olive Oil	15 mL
½ cup	*each* chopped onion and celery	125 mL
3	garlic cloves, minced	3
1	can (28 oz/796 mL) PRIMO Tomatoes	1
1	can (24 oz/680 mL) PRIMO Original Spaghetti Sauce	1
2 tsp	Worcestershire sauce	10 mL
pinch	hot pepper flakes	pinch
1	box PRIMO Jumbo Shells	1

FILLING:

2	pkgs (500 g *each*) pressed cottage cheese	2
2	eggs	2
⅓ cup	chopped walnuts	75 mL
1 cup	shredded mozzarella cheese	250 mL
½ cup	shredded Asiago cheese	125 mL
2 tbsp	*each* chopped fresh parsley and basil	25 mL
½ tsp	*each* salt and pepper	2 mL
½ cup	PRIMO 100% Grated Parmesan Cheese	125 mL

●In large saucepan, heat oil over medium heat. Add onion, celery and garlic; cook 3 minutes or until softened. Add tomatoes, spaghetti sauce, Worcestershire sauce and hot pepper flakes; bring to a boil. Reduce heat to medium-low and cook 1 hour, stirring occasionally.

●Meanwhile, in a large pot of boiling, salted water, cook pasta 18-20 minutes or until tender. Refresh in cold water and drain.

●In another large bowl, combine cottage cheese, eggs, walnuts, mozzarella, Asiago, parsley, basil, salt and pepper.

●Spread 1 cup (250 mL) of tomato sauce in bottom of each of two 13 × 9-in (3 L) baking dishes.

●Stuff each shell with 3 tbsp (45 mL) of cheese filling. Divide the stuffed shells between the 2 dishes. Pour remaining tomato sauce evenly and equally over shells; sprinkle each dish with ¼ cup (50 mL) Parmesan.

●Bake at 350°F (180°C) for 30 minutes, or until heated through.

PREPARATION TIME: 15 MINUTES
COOKING TIME: 1 HOUR
BAKING TIME: 30 MINUTES
MAKES 12 SERVINGS

WARM RATATOUILLE PASTA SALAD

1 lb	*each* **eggplant and zucchini**	450 g
1	**red bell pepper, seeded and cubed**	1
1	**onion, sliced**	1
4	**garlic cloves, minced**	4
1 tsp	**paprika**	5 mL
½ tsp	*each* **salt, pepper, dried basil and oregano**	2 mL
1	**can (28 oz/796 mL) PRIMO Tomatoes, drained and coarsely chopped**	1
3 cups	**PRIMO Bocconcini Pasta**	750 mL
	chopped fresh parsley	

● Cut eggplant and zucchini into 1-in (2.5-cm) cubes. Place in bottom of a large casserole dish. Layer with red pepper and onion.

● Sprinkle evenly with garlic, paprika, salt, pepper, basil and oregano. Spoon tomatoes evenly over top. Bake at 350°F (180°C) for 1 hour, stirring halfway through cooking time to combine.

● Meanwhile, in a large pot of boiling, salted water, cook pasta 8-10 minutes or until tender but firm. Drain pasta.

● Toss pasta with baked ratatouille. Sprinkle with parsley and serve.

PREPARATION TIME: 15 MINUTES
BAKING TIME: 1 HOUR
MAKES 4-6 SERVINGS

DELICIOUS DESSERTS

ZABAGLIONE con BISCOTTI 'S' e BACCHE

ZABAGLIONE WITH 'S' BISCUITS AND BERRIES

A simple, rich and elegant dessert.

4	egg yolks	4
¼ cup	granulated sugar	50 mL
⅓ cup	cream sherry	75 mL
1 tbsp	warm water	15 mL
2	PRIMO 'S' Biscuits, crushed	2
5 cups	quartered fresh strawberries	1.25 L

• In a heat-proof bowl, whisk together egg yolks, sugar, ¼ cup (50 mL) of sherry and warm water. Place bowl over a pot of barely simmering water. Beat with electric beaters on high for 5-7 minutes, or until mixture is thick, frothy and pale yellow.

• Toss crushed 'S' biscuits with remaining sherry. Spoon zabaglione into dessert cups and top with berries. Sprinkle with crushed biscuits and serve.

PREPARATION TIME: 15 MINUTES
COOKING TIME: 10 MINUTES
MAKES 6 SERVINGS

LOW-FAT TIRAMISÙ

2 cups	low-fat plain yogurt	500 mL
2	pkgs (150 g) PRIMO Giant Lady Fingers	2
1¼ cups	strong coffee	300 mL
2 tbsp	*each* brandy or amber rum and coffee liqueur	25 mL
1	pkg (8 oz/225 g) light cream cheese	1
1 tsp	vanilla	5 mL
1¼ tsp	unflavoured gelatin (about half of a 7 g packet)	6 mL
3 tbsp	orange juice concentrate	45 mL
½ cup	granulated sugar	125 mL
¼ cup	water	50 mL
6	egg whites	6
2 tbsp	cocoa powder	25 mL

• Place yogurt in a cheesecloth-lined sieve; set over a bowl and place in the refrigerator. Drain at least 8 hours.

• Cut 1 in (2.5 cm) off 1 end of each lady finger. Stand lady fingers upright along the edge of a 9-in (2.5 L) springform pan, rounded side against rim. Cover bottom of pan with remaining lady fingers and cut end pieces. Reserve any leftover lady finger pieces.

• Combine coffee, brandy and coffee liqueur. Drizzle 1 cup (250 mL) of coffee mixture over biscuits in pan; set aside.

• In large bowl, beat drained yogurt, cream cheese and vanilla until smooth; set aside. In small saucepan, stir together gelatin and orange juice. Heat over medium heat 2 minutes and stir into yogurt-cheese mixture.

• In a small, heavy-bottomed saucepan, stir together sugar and water. Using a candy thermometer, cook over medium-high heat until it reaches the soft ball stage (225°F/105°C). Remove from heat.

• In separate bowl, beat egg whites until foamy. Gradually pour in sugar mixture; continue beating until soft peaks form and mixture cools. Fold meringue into yogurt-cheese mixture in thirds; combine thoroughly.

• Spoon ½ of filling over coffee-soaked lady fingers. Dust with 1 tbsp (15 mL) of cocoa. Place remaining lady fingers over filling and slowly drizzle with remaining coffee mixture. Spoon remaining filling over lady finger pieces and dust with remaining cocoa. Chill at least 8 hours before serving.

TIP: Begin making this the night before you serve it so that the yogurt will have enough time to drain.

PREPARATION TIME: 30 MINUTES
COOKING TIME: 5 MINUTES
CHILLING TIME: 8 HOURS
MAKES 8-10 SERVINGS

Drain yogurt in lined sieve for at least 8 hours.

Line prepared lady fingers in springform pan, rounded side against rim.

Cover bottom of pan with remaining lady fingers and drizzle with 1 cup (250 mL) of the prepared coffee mixture.

In large bowl, beat drained yogurt, cream cheese and vanilla until smooth.

Gradually fold meringue into yogurt mixture in thirds until completely combined.

Place remaining lady fingers over filling and drizzle with coffee. Spoon with remaining filling and dust with cocoa.

Tiramisù

Tiramisù means 'pick me up' in Italian. Serve small pieces of this decadent dessert after a light dinner.

2	pkgs (150 g) PRIMO Giant Lady Fingers	2
1¾ cups	strong coffee	425 mL
2 tbsp	*each* brandy and coffee liqueur	25 mL
¼ cup	granulated sugar	50 mL
3	egg yolks	3
1	container (1 lb/450 g) Mascarpone cheese	1
1 cup	whipping cream, whipped	250 mL
2 tbsp	cocoa	25 mL

• Fit one package of lady fingers into bottom of an 11 × 7-in (2 L) baking dish.

• In a glass measuring cup, combine coffee, brandy, coffee liqueur and 1 tbsp (15 mL) sugar. Drizzle half of coffee mixture over lady fingers in dish; set aside.

• Place egg yolks and remaining sugar in a stainless steel bowl. Set bowl over hot, not boiling, water. Beat with electric beaters for 7-9 minutes, or until mixture is thick, foamy and pale yellow.

• Remove from heat and whisk in Mascarpone. Fold in ¼ of the whipped cream. Gently fold in remaining whipped cream; combine thoroughly.

• Spoon half of the Mascarpone mixture over lady fingers in dish. Dust with 1 tbsp (15 mL) of cocoa.

• Layer second package of lady fingers over filling. Drizzle remaining coffee mixture over ladyfingers. Do not worry if there is excess coffee surrounding lady fingers, it will be absorbed.

• Spoon remaining Mascarpone filling evenly over lady fingers and dust with remaining cocoa.

• Chill 4-8 hours before serving. Makes 8-10 servings.

Preparation Time: 25 minutes
Cooking Time: 10 minutes
Chilling Time: 4-8 hours

PINEAPPLE NOODLE PUDDING

1	pkg (375 g) **PRIMO Medium or Broad Egg Noodles**	1
1	can (19 oz/540 mL) crushed pineapple, drained	1
1½ cups	milk	375 mL
3	eggs, lightly beaten	3
2 tbsp	*each* sugar, honey and lemon juice	25 mL
1 tsp	vanilla	5 mL
1 cup	fresh breadcrumbs	250 mL
¼ cup	packed brown sugar	50 mL
3 tbsp	melted butter	45 mL
1 tsp	cinnamon	5 mL

● In a large pot of boiling, salted water, cook pasta 8 to 10 minutes, or until tender. Drain, rinse in cold water, drain again and set aside.

● In a large bowl, stir together pineapple, milk, eggs, sugar, honey, lemon juice and vanilla. Add noodles and combine thoroughly.

● Pour mixture into a greased 11 × 7-in (2 L) baking dish.

● In small bowl combine breadcrumbs, brown sugar, melted butter and cinnamon; sprinkle over noodle mixture.

● Bake at 350°F (180°C) for 1 hour. Let stand 10 minutes before serving.

PREPARATION TIME: 10 MINUTES
COOKING TIME: 10 MINUTES
BAKING TIME: 1 HOUR
MAKES 8 SERVINGS

APPLE CREAM LASAGNE

9	PRIMO Oven Ready Lasagne Noodles	9
⅓ cup	butter	75 mL
6	Granny Smith apples, peeled, cored and sliced	6
⅓ cup	packed brown sugar	75 mL
½ cup	toasted, chopped pecans	125 mL
2 tsp	ground cinnamon	10 mL
1	pkg (250 g) light cream cheese, softened	1
1	egg	1
1 tsp	vanilla	5 mL
1 cup	whipping cream, whipped	250 mL
½ cup	fresh breadcrumbs	125 mL
¼ cup	granulated sugar	50 mL

• Place noodles in an 11 × 7-in (2 L) baking dish, cover with warm water and soak 20 minutes. Drain and set aside.

• Meanwhile, in saucepan, melt ¼ cup (50 mL) butter over medium heat. Add apples, cover and cook 10 minutes, or until tender, stirring occasionally. Remove from heat and stir in 3 tbsp (45 mL) brown sugar, pecans and cinnamon; set aside.

• Place cream cheese and remaining brown sugar in large bowl. Beat 3 minutes or until light and fluffy. Beat in egg and vanilla. Fold whipped cream into cream cheese mixture in thirds and set aside.

• Melt remaining butter. In small bowl, combine breadcrumbs, sugar and melted butter.

• Spread half of the apple mixture in bottom of same baking dish. Layer with 3 noodles. Spread with half of cream mixture, and layer with 3 more noodles. Spread with remaining apple mixture and layer with last 3 noodles.

• Top with remaining cream mixture and sprinkle with breadcrumb mixture.

• Bake at 350°F (180°C) for 30 minutes. Let stand 20 minutes before serving.

PREPARATION TIME: 20 MINUTES
COOKING TIME: 10 MINUTES
BAKING TIME: 30 MINUTES
MAKES 8 SERVINGS

CHOCOLATE ORZO SOUFFLÉ

6 oz	bittersweet chocolate	175 g
2 tbsp	butter	25 mL
¼ cup	PRIMO Orzo	50 mL
4	egg yolks	4
8	egg whites	8
2 tbsp	granulated sugar	25 mL

- Grease a 7 × 3-in (1.5 L) soufflé dish; sprinkle sides and bottom with 2 tsp (10 mL) granulated sugar.

- Place chocolate and butter in a stainless steel bowl. Place bowl over hot, not boiling, water, until chocolate and butter have melted, stirring occasionally. Remove from heat.

- Meanwhile, in a pot of boiling, salted water, cook pasta 6 to 8 minutes or until tender. Rinse under cold water and drain.

- In small bowl, beat egg yolks 2½ minutes, or until pale yellow and thickened. Stir orzo into yolks. Fold yolk mixture into chocolate mixture.

- In a large bowl, beat together egg whites and sugar until stiff peaks form. Stir ¼ of whites into chocolate mixture and combine thoroughly. Gently fold remaining whites into chocolate mixture.

- Pour into soufflé dish. Level off top and run a small spoon around edge of dish to create an indentation around soufflé.

- Place in preheated 400°F (200°C) oven for 25-30 minutes, or until raised and firm to the touch. Serve immediately.

TIP: For individual soufflés, bake the soufflé mixture in 8 greased and sugared ramekins; reduce baking time to 10 minutes.

PREPARATION TIME: 10 MINUTES
COOKING TIME: 6-8 MINUTES
BAKING TIME: 30 MINUTES
MAKES 8 SERVINGS

Melt chocolate and butter over hot, not boiling, water, stirring until smooth.

Stir cooked orzo into egg yolks.

Fold yolk mixture into melted chocolate.

In large bowl, beat together egg whites and sugar until stiff peaks form.

Gradually fold egg whites into chocolate mixture until thoroughly combined.

Pour mixture into prepared soufflé dish. Bake for 25-30 minutes, or until raised and firm to the touch.

CREAMY RICE PUDDING

*Nothing is more comforting than the smell of rice pudding
slowly simmering on the stove.*

4 cups	milk	1 L
⅓ cup	raisins	75 mL
½ cup	PRIMO Arborio Rice	125 mL
⅓ cup	packed brown sugar	75 mL
¼ tsp	*each* ground cinnamon and salt	1 mL
1 tsp	vanilla	5 mL

• In heavy-bottomed saucepan, stir together milk, raisins, rice, sugar, cinnamon and salt. Bring to a boil over medium-high heat, stirring constantly. Reduce heat to low, cover and simmer 25 minutes, or until thickened. Stir occasionally.

• Remove lid and simmer 5 more minutes. Remove from heat and stir in vanilla. Place in individual bowls and serve.

PREPARATION TIME: 5 MINUTES
COOKING TIME: 30 MINUTES
MAKES 4-6 SERVINGS

MIXED BERRY TRIFLE

3 cups	milk	750 mL
6	egg yolks	6
¾ cup	granulated sugar	175 mL
1 tbsp	cornstarch	15 mL
1 tsp	vanilla	5 mL
1 cup	*each* blueberries, raspberries and halved strawberries	250 mL
1	pkg (150 g) PRIMO Lady Fingers, broken into pieces	1
½ cup	cream sherry	125 mL
1 cup	whipping cream	250 mL
1 tbsp	granulated sugar	15 mL

• In saucepan, heat milk over medium-high heat until it begins to simmer. Reduce heat to low.

• In a large bowl, whisk together egg yolks, sugar and cornstarch. Gradually add hot milk, whisking constantly. Return mixture to saucepan. Cook 6 minutes over medium heat until custard thickens, stirring constantly. Do not boil. Remove from heat, pour through sieve; stir in vanilla and set aside.

• In bowl, gently toss berries to combine.

• Place half of the lady fingers on bottom of an 8-cup (2 L) trifle bowl. Drizzle with ¼ cup (50 mL) of sherry and layer with half of berry mixture.

• Spoon half of custard evenly over berries. Repeat layers. Cover and chill 4 hours or overnight.

• Whip cream and sugar until stiff peaks form. Spread or pipe whipped cream on top of trifle and serve.

PREPARATION TIME: 20 MINUTES
COOKING TIME: 10 MINUTES
REFRIGERATION TIME: 4 HOURS
MAKES 6 TO 8 SERVINGS

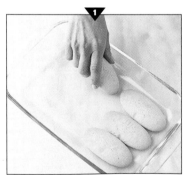

Line a baking dish with lady fingers.

Brush lady fingers with ¹/₃ cup (75 mL) of pineapple juice.

Layer peaches and pineapple over lady fingers.

PINEAPPLE PEACH TREAT

1 cup	**PRIMO Orzo**	250 mL
1	**pkg (5.3 oz/150 g) PRIMO Giant Lady Fingers**	1
1	**can (14 oz/398 mL) crushed pineapple, well-drained, reserving juice**	1
1	**can (28 oz/796 mL) sliced peaches, drained**	1
1 cup	**ricotta cheese**	250 mL
1¾ cups	**cold milk**	425 mL
1	**pkg (4-serving size) instant vanilla pudding**	1
1 cup	**whipping cream, whipped**	250 mL

- In a large pot of boiling, salted water, cook pasta 6-8 minutes, or until tender but firm. Drain, rinse with cold water, drain again and set aside.

- Meanwhile, line an 11 × 7-in (2 L) baking dish with lady fingers. Cut lady fingers if necessary.

- Brush lady fingers with ⅓ cup (75 mL) of reserved pineapple juice. Discard any leftover juice.

- Reserve ½ cup (125 mL) of sliced peaches. Layer remaining peaches over lady fingers; sprinkle with pineapple.

- In a blender, purée ricotta until smooth. Place ricotta, milk and instant pudding in a large bowl. Using an electric beater, beat 2 minutes or until thoroughly combined. Stir in cooked orzo.

- Pour mixture over pineapple-peach layer. Chill 1-8 hours. Garnish with whipped cream and reserved peaches, and serve.

PREPARATION TIME: 20 MINUTES
COOKING TIME: 6-8 MINUTES
CHILLING TIME: 1-8 HOURS
MAKES 10-12 SERVINGS

In large bowl, beat together ricotta, milk, and instant pudding until smooth.

Stir cooked orzo into pudding mixture.

Pour pudding mixture over pineapple layer and chill 1-8 hours.

CANNELLONI CHEESE BLINTZES WITH STRAWBERRY COULIS

16	**PRIMO Oven Ready Cannelloni Noodles**	16
2 tbsp	**cold butter, cut into cubes**	25 mL
	powdered sugar and light sour cream	

CHEESE FILLING:

1 cup	**low-fat ricotta cheese**	250 mL
1	**pkg (8 oz/225 g) light cream cheese, softened**	1
3 tbsp	**granulated sugar**	45 mL
1	**egg**	1
1 tsp	*each* **finely grated lemon rind and lemon juice**	5 mL

STRAWBERRY COULIS:

¼ cup	*each* **granulated sugar and water**	50 mL
2 cups	**fresh or frozen strawberries**	500 mL
½ tsp	**lemon juice**	2 mL

• In a large pot of boiling, salted water, cook cannelloni 10-12 minutes or until tender. Drain and refresh under cold water. Slice each tube along the length and lay flat on clean tea towel; set aside.

• In a blender, purée ricotta until smooth. Place ricotta, cream cheese, sugar, egg, lemon rind and juice in bowl. Using an electric beater, beat until thoroughly combined.

• Place noodles on work surface. Divide cheese filling evenly between noodles; spread on long side of each noodle. Roll up jelly-roll style, and place in a buttered, 13 × 9-in (3 L) baking dish. Dot with cubed butter. Cover with foil and bake at 400°F (200°C) for 20 minutes, or until heated through.

• Meanwhile, in a small saucepan, combine sugar and water; cook over medium heat until sugar dissolves. Stir in strawberries and lemon juice and toss to coat. In blender, purée strawberry mixture until smooth.

• Spoon strawberry coulis on dessert plates and place two blintzes on each. Dust with powdered sugar and top with sour cream. Serve warm garnished with mint leaves.

TIP: You can substitute raspberries for strawberries in this dessert, but make sure to adjust the sugar accordingly. Can be prepared up to 8 hours ahead of time and baked just before serving.

PREPARATION TIME: 25 MINUTES
COOKING TIME: 10 MINUTES
BAKING TIME: 20 MINUTES
MAKES 8 SERVINGS

INDEX

A

Aglio e Olio, Spaghetti 115
Alfredo, Fettuccine 124
Alfredo, Light Fettuccine 124
Amaretto Squash Soup
   (Zuppa di Zucca all'Amaretto) 46
Amatriciana, Penne all' 86
Antipasto 27
Apple Cream Lasagne 180
Arrabbiata, Penne all' 115

B

BEAN
   Black Bean Soup 45
   Insalata di Fagioli con Tonno
     (Bean Salad with Tuna) 52
   Italian Bean Dip 33
   Pasta e Fagioli (Pasta and Bean Soup) 50
   Zuppa Toscana di Fagioli e Pasta
     (Tuscan Bean-Pasta Soup) 42
BEEF
   Beef and Pepper Ragout 137
   Beef Stroganoff 72
   Pasta with Stir-Fried Beef and Vegetables 85
   Romano Cheese and Basil Penne with Beef 76
   Stifado (Greek Beef Stew) 142
Black Bean Soup 45
BOCCONCINI PASTA
   Bocconcini with Grilled Chicken,
     Sun-Dried Tomatoes and Mushrooms 70
   Bocconcini with Roasted Bell Peppers
     and Mushrooms 105
Bolognese Sauce 144
Bruschetta al Pomodoro
   (Tomato Bruschetta) 34

C

Caesar Pasta Salad with Roasted
   Garlic Dressing 58
CANNELLONI
   Cannelloni Cheese Blintzes
     with Strawberry Coulis 188
Carbonara, Spaghetti alla 82
Cheese-Stuffed Shells 171
CHICK-PEAS
   Chick-pea Hummus 22
   East Indian Curried Chick-peas 113
   Herbed Pasta and Chick-peas 104
CHICKEN
   Bocconcini with Grilled Chicken,
     Sun-Dried Tomatoes and Mushrooms 70
   Chicken Noodle Soup 45
   Chicken Parmesan 162

Chicken Rice Soup 44
Chicken Tettrazini 149
Chicken and Vegetable Pennine 80
Coq au Vin 141
Curried Chicken Pasta Salad 62
Pasta-Stuffed Roast Chicken 157
Pollo alla Cacciatora (Chicken Cacciatore) 135
Thai-Style Coconut Chicken Stir-Fry 74
Chocolate Orzo Soufflé 182
Cioppino-Style Linguine 94
Colby & Gouda Penne Salad 67
Coq au Vin 141
Creamy Rice Pudding 184
Creamy Seafood Linguine with Lemon 96
Creamy Tomato Vodka Sauce 127
Crostini all'Aglio (Garlic Crostini) 19
Curried Chicken Pasta Salad 62
Curried Wild Rice, Orzo and Lentil Salad 63

E

East Indian Curried Chick-peas 113

F

Fast and Easy Turkey Stir-Fry 76
FETTUCCINE
   Fettuccine Alfredo 124
   Fettuccine with Smoked Salmon
     and Asparagus 97
   Light Fettuccine Alfredo 124
Focaccia 20
Funghi Marinati (Marinated Mushrooms) 16

G

Garden Tomato and Herb Sauce 108
Greek Medley Salad 56
Grilled Ratatouille 30
Grilled Vegetable Pasta Salad 57

H

Herbed Pasta and Chick-peas 104
Hot Artichoke Dip 19
Hummus, Chick-pea 22

I

Insalata di Fagioli con Tonno
   (Bean Salad with Tuna) 52
Italian Bean Dip 33

L

LASAGNE
   Apple Cream Lasagne 180

Lasagne con Carne (Lasagne with Meat) 160
Lasagne Roll-ups 154
Seafood Lasagne 146
Zucchini and Eggplant Lasagne 168
Light Fettuccine Alfredo 124
LINGUINE
Cioppino-Style Linguine 94
Creamy Seafood Linguine with Lemon 96
Linguine con Salsa al Gorgonzola (Linguine
    with Gorgonzola Cream Sauce) 129
Linguine al Pesto (Linguine with Pesto) 108
Linguine alla Puttanesca 117
Linguine alla Romana 77
Linguine alle Vongole in Salsa Bianca
    (Linguine with White Clam Sauce) 90
Linguine alle Vongole in Salsa Rossa
    (Linguine with Red Clam Sauce) 91
Linguine in Wild Mushroom Sauce 130
Linguine with Caramelized Onions 118
Low-Fat Tiramisù 176

M
MACARONI
Old-Fashioned Macaroni and Cheese 167
MANICOTTI
Swiss Manicotti 159
Marinated Goat Cheese 16
Mediterranean Dip 36
Minestrone 41
Mini Pizzas 26
Mixed Berry Trifle 185
Mushroom Risotto 107
Mussel Soup (Zuppa di Cozze) 48

N
New Spaghetti and Meatballs 138
Niçoise Pasta Salad 64

O
Old-Fashioned Macaroni and Cheese 167
Olive Marinate (Marinated Olives) 16
ORZO
Chocolate Orzo Soufflé 182
Curried Wild Rice, Orzo and Lentil Salad 63
Osso Buco 132

P
Pad Thai 98
Pasta ai Quattro Formaggi
    (Pasta with Four Cheeses) 126
Pasta Chips 33
Pasta con Tonno e Olive
    (Pasta with Tuna and Olives) 100
Pasta e Fagioli (Pasta and Bean Soup) 50
Pasta Primavera 102
Pasta with Stir-Fried Beef and Vegetables 85

Pasta-Stuffed Roast Chicken 157
Pastitsio 164
PENNE
Colby and Gouda Penne Salad 67
Penne all'Amatriciana 86
Penne all'Arrabbiata 115
Romano Cheese and Basil Penne
    with Beef 76
PENNINE
Chicken and Vegetable Pennine 80
Pennine Asparagus Salad
    with Parsley Pesto 60
Pesto, Linguine al 108
Pineapple Noodle Pudding 179
Pineapple Peach Treat 187
Pita Crisps 22
POLENTA
Quadratini di Polenta Gratinata con
    Gorgonzola (Grilled Polenta Squares
    with Gorgonzola) 24
Polenta 122
Polenta Pasticciata (Polenta with Sausages
    and Cheese) 150
Pollo alla Cacciatora (Chicken Cacciatore) 135
Primavera, Pasta 102
Puttanesca, Linguine alla 117

Q
Quadratini di Polenta Gratinata con Gorgonzola
    (Grilled Polenta Squares with Gorgonzola) 24
Quattro Formaggi, Pasta ai 126

R
RICE
Chicken Rice Soup 44
Creamy Rice Pudding 184
Supplì di Riso (Rice Croquettes) 29
Risotto alla Milanese (Saffron Rice) 107
Roasted Red Pepper Dip 19
Romana, Linguine alla 77
Romano Cheese and Basil Penne with Beef 76
Rotini with Swiss Chard,
    Pine Nuts and Raisins 119

S
Salsa per Spaghetti Casereccia
    (Homemade Spaghetti Sauce) 136
Savoury Noodle Kugel 166
Seafood Lasagne 146
Shrimp Vegetable Stir-Fry 88
SPAGHETTI
New Spaghetti and Meatballs 138
Spaghetti Aglio e Olio
    (Spaghetti with Garlic and Oil) 115
Spaghetti al Baccalà
    (Spaghetti with Salt Cod) 92

Spaghetti alla Mozzarella
(Mozzarella Spaghetti)   129
Spaghetti alla Carbonara   82
Spaghetti with Cauliflower   110
Salsa per Spaghetti Casereccia
(Homemade Spaghetti Sauce)   136
SPAGHETTINI
Spaghettini with Eggplant and Tomato   120
Spaghettini with Sun-Dried Tomato Pesto   112
Spicy Sausage and Greens Pasta   83
Stifado (Greek Beef Stew)   142
Stracciatella   40
Stroganoff, Beef   72
Supplì di Riso (Rice Croquettes)   29
Sweet and Sour Pork Stir-Fry
with Noodle Pancakes   79
Swiss Manicotti   159

T
Tex-Mex Pasta Casserole   152
Thai Pasta Shrimp and Vegetable Salad   55
Thai-Style Coconut Chicken Stir-Fry   74
Tiramisù   178
Tiramisù, Low-Fat   176
TOMATO
Bruschetta al Pomodoro
(Tomato Bruschetta)   34
Creamy Tomato Vodka Sauce   127

Spaghettini with Eggplant and Tomato   120
Tomato-Basil Pasta Salad
with Goat Cheese   52
Tomato Risotto   107
Two-Mushroom Tomato Pasta Toss   73
Tri-Colour Pasta Salad   68
Tuna Casserole   161
TURKEY
Fast and Easy Turkey Stir-Fry   76
Turkey Waldorf Pasta Salad   67
Tuscan Bean-Pasta Soup (Zuppa Toscana di
Fagioli e Pasta)   42
Two-Mushroom Tomato Pasta Toss   73

V-W
Vegetarian Pistou   38
Warm Ratatouille Pasta Salad   172
White Bean Bruschetta   34

Z
Zabaglione con Biscotti 'S' e Bacche
(Zabaglione with 'S' Biscuits and Berries)   174
Zucchini and Eggplant Lasagne   168
Zuppa di Cozze (Mussel Soup)   48
Zuppa di Zucca all'Amaretto
(Amaretto Squash Soup)   46
Zuppa Toscana di Fagioli e Pasta
(Tuscan Bean-Pasta Soup)   42